WRITING HARD STORIES

WRITING HARD STORIES

CELEBRATED MEMOIRISTS
WHO SHAPED
ART FROM TRAUMA

MELANIE BROOKS

Beacon Press · Boston

BEACON PRESS
Boston, Massachusetts
www.beacon.org

Beacon Press books
are published under the auspices of
the Unitarian Universalist Association of Congregations.

25 24 23   8 7 6 5

This book is printed on acid-free paper that meets the uncoated paper
ANSI/NISO specifications for permanence as revised in 1992.

Text design and composition by Kim Arney

Versions of two of these profiles were previously published: Joan Wickersham's
in *Solstice Literary Magazine* (Summer 2015) and Suzanne Strempek Shea's in
the *Stonecoast Review* (Fall 2015).

Names: Brooks, Melanie, author.
Title: Writing hard stories : celebrated memoirists who shaped art from
    trauma / Melanie Brooks.
Description: Boston : Beacon Press, 2017.
Identifiers: LCCN 2016023104 (print) | LCCN 2016040221 (ebook) |
    ISBN 9780807078815 (paperback) | ISBN 9780807078822 (e-book)
Subjects: LCSH: Autobiography. | Autobiography—Authorship. |
    Biography as a literary form. | Psychic trauma in literature. | BISAC:
    LANGUAGE ARTS & DISCIPLINES / Composition & Creative
    Writing. | BIOGRAPHY & AUTOBIOGRAPHY / Personal Memoirs. |
    LANGUAGE ARTS & DISCIPLINES / Authorship.
Classification: LCC CT25 .B75 2017 (print) | LCC CT25 (ebook) |
    DDC 808.06/692—dc23
LC record available at https://lccn.loc.gov/2016023104

For Chris, you are my companion
through life's hardest and best parts

·

For Will and Lily, you are the best parts

·

And for all those with difficult stories to tell,
you are not alone

Contents

Introduction

Near the beginning of my master of fine arts degree, a friend introduced me to a fellow student while we sat waiting for a faculty presentation to begin.

"What's your genre?" he asked.

"Creative nonfiction," I replied.

"So I guess you'll write about your father and then cry," he said.

I could see he was joking. He didn't strike me as a mean guy. But I was new to this writing program scene. Uncertain about whether I belonged or not. Whether the story I had to tell, which *was* about my father and often did make me cry, could adequately compare to the work around me. His glib remark tore into all of my deepest insecurities.

"I guess so," I said trying to keep my voice steady and turning away before he could see the unwanted tears that stung my eyes.

Without intending to, this guy had initiated me to an undercurrent that I've discovered is not uncommon in literary circles and workshop settings: a discomfort with the very real emotion that underlies writing about sensitive subject matter.

It's a discomfort that leads some workshop facilitators to stop conversations about the actual content of student pieces with words like "Let's keep our focus on craft here." A discomfort that has made me, on more than one occasion, feel ashamed of the tears that sometimes surface with discussion of my work and jokingly label myself "The Crier" to put others at ease when they're confronted by my pain. A discomfort that gave one woman in a workshop the audacity to say, in a tone so beyond pretentious I can't find a word for it, "The question you want to ask yourself is 'Am I just simply writing in my journal or am I trying to create *literature?*'"

This idea that somehow emotionally charged, often traumatic personal stories presented as nonfiction are masquerading as literature has accompanied the recent evolution of the memoir genre. It's also what compels many authors to qualify their work as "*literary* memoir," so as not to be lumped in with what *New York Times* book critic Neil Genzlinger calls "this absurdly bloated genre" or what his counterpart, Michiko Kakutani, claims is "propelled by the belief that confession is therapeutic and therapy is redemptive and redemption somehow equals art."

And it's an idea that has so often left me alone to flounder in the psychological turmoil and vulnerability of revisiting the grief and hurt and confusion of my own hard story, because people habitually back away from this inevitable offshoot of doing the kind of writing that requires us to dig deep. I needed to find the people who'd be willing to step closer.

So, on a day in March 2013, when several inches of freshly fallen snow blanket Boston's streets, I feel a little claustrophobic because of the press of people crowding the front tables of the large conference room inside the John B. Hynes Veterans Memorial Convention Center. In a throng of other eager and hopeful writers attending this particular session at the annual conference for the Association of Writers and Writing Programs (AWP), I wait for my turn to speak to author and poet Kim Stafford. My mind tumbles over the question I am poised to ask. Jostled forward, I meet Stafford's expectant gaze at the same time that an unexpected nervousness floods my body. My palms feel clammy, my throat tight. I don't give myself time to think before I blurt out, "How did you do it?"

As soon as the rush of words leaves my lips and I see Stafford's jaw tighten before his face softens into a patient and teacherly expression, I realize my mistake. He thinks I am asking him about craft. The question I'd prepared in my head had morphed into those dreaded words most published writers loathe to hear. The ones that ask for the formula to literary success.

"Just keep doing the work," he says, his kind eyes crinkling at the corners. "Keep drawing on the tools you have and do the work." Before I can reboot my brain and self-correct, I've lost not only Stafford's attention but also my space in line. The people behind bump me to the side. Disappointment washes over me. Utterly deflated, I step through the wide door into a hallway crammed with moving bodies and raucous chatter.

I'd asked the completely wrong question.

I am midway through the first semester of my MFA, a newbie to this conference where twelve-thousand-plus authors, teachers, students, publishers, editors, and agents meander and mingle in the hallways; travel up and down the escalators in a never-ending human stream to attend readings, panels, and keynote addresses; and wander around with an equal mixture of euphoria and terror at the sheer magnitude of this gathering of creative people.

It's Day 2 of the four-day conference, and I have yet to be initiated to the number-one rule of these kinds of events: pace yourself. I'm at the brink of physical and mental exhaustion after attending seven pretty intense panel presentations, and feel that at any moment I might collapse into a weepy heap on the floor.

The letdown of my missed opportunity with Kim Stafford isn't helping.

The description of Stafford's panel, "Writing Past the End," in the three-hundred-page AWP program that weighs down my bag, caught my attention with these words: "In this panel we look squarely at paralyzing stories that must be told. The writer tilts the mirror to see inside a hidden life and embrace the dark [. . .] seeking grace through story in spite of all."

For two months, I've been trying to write my way into my piece of a family story that has pushed to be heard for years. When I was thirteen years old, my father, a distinguished general and thoracic surgeon, was infected with HIV from a contaminated blood transfusion while undergoing open-heart surgery. The year was 1985, and ignorance and hysteria about AIDS were at their height. In Canada, where we lived, rumors swirled about publicly identifying and quarantining AIDS patients and their families. Believing he had only months of his life left and afraid of the stigma of this disease, my father decided to keep his illness a secret. No one imagined he would live another ten years. But he did. And for ten years, through my adolescence and early adulthood, the secret of his disease and the specter of catastrophe that inevitably loomed ahead defined my life.

Journeying honestly into this hard story and unearthing the ongoing grief of losing my dad to AIDS in 1995 has been agonizing. And terrifying. And, more often than not, paralyzing.

The panelists—Kim Stafford, Gregory Orr, Nan Cuba, and Jill Bialosky—had all written books that enter the aftermath of losing a sibling to either suicide or violent death. They shared their stories of bringing their traumas to the page, and all spoke directly to the feelings of fear and risk and vulnerability inherent in the process. But it was Stafford, in particular, who described his experience writing his memoir, *One Hundred Tricks Every Boy Can Do: How My Brother Disappeared*, as "setting down a difficult burden" whose story I felt most drawn to.

Stafford had written an essay, "How a Book Can Set You Free," about what it felt like to get the galley copy of his memoir in the mail. With a slight tremble in his voice, Stafford read a passage from the essay: "I cried for him as I read. He caught me. But his story was no longer a stone harnessed to my heart. My heart was not carrying him any more. I had been released from this lonesome duty, for his story was in a book in my hands."

My eyes filled. This is what I want, I thought. I want my father's story, *my* story, to be something other than this crushing weight of grief that I carry so close. I want it to be something different. Something meaningful. But my fear of really examining that grief is standing in my way.

What I really needed to understand, I realized then, was how these writers had managed to get from the distressing place where I was mired in my writing to where they now were in theirs.

But when I got my chance to question Stafford after the presentation, I'd blown it.

When I asked him "How did you do it?" I didn't want to know about the literary techniques that Stafford employed. I didn't want to know the elements of style and language and tone that he drew on to allow his words to resonate on the page. I knew he couldn't give me those particulars; I'm far enough along in my own writing and my teaching of writing to understand that those things are unique to the individual and the particular story. What I'd wanted to know, with a desperation that will attach itself to me and settle in for the duration of the conference and then trail me back to my writing desk and into the next few months of writing and staring at the blinking cursor on my laptop's blank screen, was this:

How did Stafford *survive*?

I have an entire bookshelf of memoirs that I've been collecting and reading for my MFA program: Memoirs that tell hard stories. Memoirs about child abuse, about battling illness, traumatic injuries, neglect and addiction and violence and fear. Memoirs about painful searches for identity and belonging. Memoirs about the death of a beloved someone: friend, parent, spouse, lover, sibling. A child. Memoirs that journey through moments of unimaginable grief and life-changing trauma.

How did any of these writers survive? I start reading interviews with some of the authors, selfishly hoping to learn about how they'd also been traumatized in the process of writing their stories, how they'd spent a lot of time crying, how they'd been paralyzed over the keyboard, how they'd had to find a good therapist.

Instead, I encounter a wide range of interviews that talk book, that talk craft, that talk personal writing habits, but steer completely clear of the high emotional stakes that accompany writing an honest memoir. These interviews were interesting, but they left me craving so much more.

I'd read these memoirs. Identified closely with the pain in their pages. And that's what I want, no, *need*, to know about. "How did it feel to write the gut-wrenching scenes in *Heaven's Coast* of watching Wally's AIDS-ravaged body disappear before your eyes?" I want to ask Mark Doty. "What was it like to make the decision to reveal the truth about your dad's shortcomings as a father in the pages of *Townie*?" I long to ask Andre Dubus III. "How did you cope with the shame of revisiting your poor decisions when you wrote *Street Shadows*?" I wish to question Jerald Walker. "Did you worry you were letting pieces of your son go when you shaped the story of his life and death into *Jesse: A Mother's Story*?" I wonder about Marianne Leone.

I keep turning these questions and so many more over and over again in my head, and an idea starts to percolate. Why don't *I* ask them? Why not try for a do-over of my failed attempt with Kim Stafford at AWP? I could write to these writers. I could write to them all and ask them to sit down with me. To sit down with me and describe what it was like as they began venturing into the dangerous territory of their hard stories. I'd ask them how they survived their own feelings of fear and doubt and sadness. I'd ask them, and maybe, just maybe, their answers would convince me to keep going.

And so, I do.

In March 2014, almost a year to the day after my AWP debacle, I embark on a quest. I prepare a list of questions. These questions are not about craft. We do a good job of talking craft in writing programs, workshops, and conferences. I want to explore the territory I think we tend to shy away from discussing: the psychological impact of telling our stories. My questions intentionally begin with these kinds of words: What was it like? How did it feel? I'm unearthing the emotional toll of reaching into our memories and pulling our traumas to the surface. I'm searching for the place where their experiences meet mine, hoping to discover that I'm not really as alone as I feel.

Over the next two years, I will drive from my home in Nashua, New Hampshire, to various cities and towns in Massachusetts— Boston, Cambridge, Bondsville, Kingston—as well as Portland, Maine, and East Hampton, New York. I'll take the train to New York City, and I'll fly to Miami, Minneapolis, Los Angeles, and Washington, DC.

I will be invited to drink tea, share meals, and visit homes.

And I will engage in intimate conversations with eighteen of the most generous people I've ever met. People who don't back away from exposing the vulnerabilities inherent when writing hard stories. With humility and candor, they will share what it was like for them to put words to their stories. I'll hear about their tears. Their false starts. Their failures. Their moments of grief and rage and doubt and despair. They'll detail their own treks into the darkest places of their memories and the things that helped them to keep going when that darkness felt paralyzing. And then they'll detail the breakthrough moments of unlocking their stories and making them something meaningful to send out into the world. I'll hear about their feelings of accomplishment. Of gratitude. Relief.

These beautiful conversations are contained in the pages of this book. Each one has something to teach emerging writers, established writers, teachers of writing, memoir readers, and those who have faced or are facing difficult experiences.

Author C. S. Lewis reputedly once said, "We read to know we are not alone." Humans are naturally drawn to the stories of how others cope with loss and adversity because none of us escapes this world without enduring some ourselves.

I wrote this book to be a trusted companion to walk alongside writers who have difficult, but necessary and important, stories to tell. The knowledge that we are not alone in the inevitable challenges that emerge when we venture to shape hard life into beautiful art is perhaps the strongest mooring a writer can find. But I hope, too, that this book will be a mooring for those who cannot tell their stories or who have simply been moved by the stories these gifted writers have told them.

CHAPTER I

Andre Dubus III

· *Townie*

Until now, even though I live less than twenty-five minutes
away, I've never visited St. Anselm's College in Manchester,
New Hampshire. But on this Tuesday at the end of March, when
overcast skies and chilly temps still forecast the possibility of a
late-season snowfall, I drive up the curving lane to the hilltop
from which the picturesque campus overlooks New Hampshire's
"Queen City." I am amazed that this small Catholic liberal arts
college, with its red-brick buildings and tree-studded landscape,
is only minutes away from our state's most populated city.

St. A's is where Andre Dubus III, celebrated author of fiction
and nonfiction, has generously made time to meet with me to talk
about his memoir, *Townie*, in between his guest appearance in a
creative writing class and a public talk and reading. He is fully
entrenched in a hectic tour schedule for his latest book, *Dirty
Love*, a collection of four stories linked by theme—the disorient-
ing nature of love—and setting—a small, New England coastal
town. Since the beginning of March, he's given readings in New
York City, Indianapolis, Tucson, Wellesley, Massachusetts, and
Southington, Connecticut. That Dubus has carved out deliberate

space for me, a stranger who sent him a pitch via e-mail, already points to the bigheartedness of his spirit.

I wait for him in the school's coffee shop near the far window at a table that gives me a clear view of the door. The place is quiet at two o'clock in the afternoon, except for a guy cleaning the floor, his shoulders hunched as he pushes an industrial-sized vacuum.

When the door does open, a gray-haired gentleman with glasses and a digital SLR camera slung around his neck approaches my table. In my pre-interview research, I've seen numerous photos of Andre Dubus III and know that this man is not Dubus. The beeline he makes to me implies a connection, though. "Melanie?" he asks, and introduces himself as Ed Gleason, a professor of English at St. Anselm's. "Andre just had to run to his car," he tells me. "He'll be here in a few minutes." I recognize that he must be Dubus's host for the day's activities, and since I'm part of those activities, he's now my host, too.

While we wait, Gleason gushes about Dubus's visit to his creative writing class and how amazing it was to have him work with his students. "He's just so good!" he exclaims. "They loved him." I imagine they would. Dubus is a *New York Times* best-selling author. His *House of Sand and Fog*, published in 1999, was a National Book Award finalist, picked for Oprah's Book Club, and made into an Academy Award–nominated film in 2003. He's writer in residence at the University of Massachusetts–Lowell, where he teaches full time. Gleason and his students are not the only ones enamored with Andre Dubus III's achievements.

We both turn when the door opens again, and, this time, I recognize Dubus as the handsome, fifty-something (fifty-four, I'll learn) man in the long overcoat striding our way. He has dark, wavy hair salted with traces of gray, a strong jaw, kind eyes, and a ready smile. He projects an air of self-assurance but not arrogance. An effortless charisma that warrants attention.

He greets me warmly with a firm handshake. We each grab a hot drink, and then Gleason guides us out the door and down a paved pathway to another campus building where he's thoughtfully arranged a more comfortable and intimate venue for my conversation with Dubus. Gleason ushers us into a stunning room with high ceilings and natural light that filters through a wall of windows. A rectangle table sits in the middle of the room surrounded by cushioned chairs.

As Dubus removes his overcoat and I'm about to set my bag down, Gleason uncaps his camera lens and asks if he can snap a quick photo of Dubus.

"Sure," Dubus responds. "Where do you want me?"

Gleason points to the center chair at the table. "Your father sat in this very spot when he spoke here years ago. Would you mind?"

While Gleason sets up the shot and asks Dubus to pose exactly as his father had, I cringe just a little. Of course, it would be impossible for Andre Dubus III to escape his literary heritage; he shares a name with his late father, renowned master of the short story. But my personal take is that when you've achieved the kind of critical acclaim that Andre Dubus III has achieved in his professional career, rather than being cast in the shadow of your father, you deserve your own pose and your own chair.

"It happens all the time," he'll tell me when the topic of following in his father's literary footsteps inevitably comes up in our conversation, and I mention the picture taking. "I'm really okay with it now."

The *now* inserted into that sentence says a lot about the redemptive evolution of Dubus's relationship with his father. A father-son relationship that is the beating heart of his memoir, *Townie*. A father-son relationship that he resisted putting into the book for a long time because he, the son, had minimized its impact. A father-son relationship that he finally had to pull out of the dark and hold up to the light if he was going to tell his truth on the page. "When I went back to the memory of my youth, my father's absence in our daily lives became a huge presence in our lives. I couldn't deny it," he'll explain later in the interview when we discuss some of the obstacles he faced while writing his memoir.

When we relax into our chairs after Gleason leaves the room, though, it's Dubus, not me, who starts the conversation. "So tell me about you and writing," he says. His question catches me off-guard because that's what I'm supposed to be asking him. But as he leans in, looks me straight in the eye, props his elbows on the table, and takes a sip of coffee, I recognize he's not just being polite. He really wants to know.

So I tell him. I tell him that I've been writing, but only in fits and spurts, since I was an undergrad. I tell him about my years of teaching and raising a family and every other excuse I used to avoid looking at the real story that waited for my attention. I tell him about starting my MFA and feeling that the time had come to stop making excuses. And I tell him that even though I truly believe the time is now, writing my story continues to be one of the most difficult paths I've ever traveled.

Dubus poses a question every now and then, but mostly he just listens. When I finish what amounts to about a ten-minute monologue, he sits back, his gaze thoughtful, and says, "When you are writing a memoir, it's your time. It's your time to go back. And don't feel like you need to apologize for taking the time. You are being called, I would submit to you, by the younger Melanie, by the girl Melanie, by the young woman Melanie."

Dubus is describing exactly the unrelenting pull I've felt to bring my story to the page. He gets it.

"Only you will be able to tell you if you are ready to step into this material, but without really knowing you, the vibe I get tells me you are," he says. "In my memoir, I had to get forty years down the road from some of that stuff, thirty years minimum, to be able to tell it honestly."

With those words, Dubus launches, unprompted, into the conversation I'm here for: the story of how he managed to write *Townie*. He talks now, and I listen. I barely ask any of the questions I've prepared, but our initial discussion has given him the context to discern the answers I need.

Dubus calls *Townie* his "accidental memoir." In 2008, he'd just finished his novel *The Garden of Last Days* and had a contract with his publisher for a collection of personal essays. He started writing a particular essay about baseball, a game he's grown to love over the years as his two sons have climbed the ranks of the sport. When he was a young boy, though, Dubus really knew nothing about baseball. "The question fueling the essay was this: How, as a kid, did I miss this game I now love so much? What was I doing instead?" He explores this question in a piece he wrote for *River Teeth* journal after *Townie*'s publication called "Writing and Publishing a Memoir: What in the Hell Have I Done?," winner of a 2014 Pushcart Prize. The editors had asked him to write about the differences between writing nonfiction and fiction. When we first sit down at the table, Dubus hands me a copy of this essay. "I printed it off for you this morning thinking it might be helpful for your project." I'm touched by the forethought in the gesture.

"I believe," Dubus says, taking a bit of a tangential turn from telling me about the baseball essay, "that most of us can pretty much tell people our story." He pauses, and when he speaks again, his tone is more intense. "But just because we know what happened, doesn't mean we know *what the hell* happened." He explains that we can all create a time line for the chronology of events in our stories. It's the figuring out the meaning within that chronology and understanding its impact that make the writing part challenging.

"When you look at the word *remember*, the opposite of re-member is not *forget*, it's *dismember*. Chop, chop, chop." He slices the air with his hand. "*Remember* means to put back together again." And it's here that Dubus circles back to the baseball essay he was writing in 2008.

"When my son Austin was going into the nine-year-old league, I volunteered to coach but forgot that I knew nothing about baseball." He laughs. "There'd be many moments when I'd give a kid advice, but it was the wrong advice, because I didn't actually know how to play the game." The irony in this disconnect led to some funny moments that seemed like good material for his essay, so he started writing. As he wrote, though, he began to really look at his own lack of experience with the game as a child.

"I remember driving by a Little League field when I was about nine or ten, and I didn't know what it was. I didn't play ball. I didn't watch ball. I didn't see it on TV. I did not know what a Little League field was." As these small pieces of memory took shape, Dubus had to try to put them together. And putting them together meant looking deeply into a childhood that caused him, among so many other things, to completely miss out on America's favorite pastime.

This putting-together process of all the things he was doing instead of playing baseball took Dubus on the uncharted path of writing *Townie*. In the *River Teeth* essay, Dubus provides his own synopsis of the book:

> It's a memoir, a memory of a time in my existence that has a shape and narrative arc of its own, the way so many moments of our lives do: my young mother and father divorced; we lived in poverty and my mother was left to raise the four of us as best she could; we moved from one cheap rented house to the next, and I was always the new kid and I got bullied till one day I began to fight back till that was all I ever seemed to do and I was on a road that would either get me killed or put in prison; and it was my finding creative writing that put me on a more peaceful and constructive path.

It's an accurate summary, but it doesn't quite capture the fullness of the haunting narrative that is both shockingly violent and gut-wrenchingly tender, woven with honesty, self-exposure, and compassion. A narrative that lingers with its readers, cycling around in their thoughts, long after its final words.

Dubus tells me now that even though he came to the point where he knew he was writing a lot more than an essay on baseball, he still resisted the idea. "I didn't want to write a memoir," he confesses. "I didn't want to." Even when he admitted to himself that this was actually his own true story, he still had it in his mind that he was going to write this book a certain way. He'd write about his insider experience with street fighting. He'd write about himself. He'd write about his own flaws. He wasn't going to write about anybody else, though. "Who am I to write about my family?" he asked when his editor kindly pointed out the glaring absence of anyone he actually lived with during these years of his adolescence. He explains that what he discovered is "just because we want to write something a certain way, doesn't mean it wants to be written that way."

Dubus is a self-proclaimed "quote king," and during our conversation, I notice he often peppers his own insights with remembered lines from other writers, including one from Tobias Wolff. "'Memory has its own story to tell,'" Dubus says. "You've got to paint your story with a deeply subjective brush."

According to Dubus, the best way to create that painting is by approaching the story with genuine curiosity. "I have this theory that what distinguishes decent writing from good writing and good writing from great writing is just how rigorous the writer was in his or her curiosity, just how authentic and sincere they were. In the A-plus books, the writer went to the bottom of the experience and what did he or she find? More bottomlessness. There are no answers, there are only questions."

Townie is one of those A-plus books. Dubus does not gloss over the rage-fueled violence that ruled his life as a young man growing up in the mill town Haverhill, Massachusetts. He doesn't contrive a resolution. Instead, he carefully peels back the layers of his experience and answers what he believes is the only question that really matters for writers of memoir: "What was it really like?"

He doesn't downplay how very difficult answering that question can actually be, especially when you are writing a story that intersects with other people's lives. Dubus worried about invading the privacy of his siblings. Of his mother. Of his father. He worried about his brushstrokes casting them in an unfavorable light and crystallizing them at a point in time that left no room for fluidity. He couldn't help feeling that he was betraying them.

Which is why, he tells me, the first draft of the book that his editor saw left out everything about all of those people he lived with.

When those fears of betrayal restricted his writing, a conversation with his friend the fiction writer Richard Russo, who would, in 2012, go on to publish his own memoir, *Elsewhere*, gave Dubus just the perspective he needed to work through them. "He said the most helpful thing, and this might be all you need to hear today." Dubus leans in closer to me from his spot across the table. "He said, 'If this were me, I would ask myself: Am I trying to hurt anyone with this book? If the answer is yes, then I wouldn't write it, or I would write it, but I wouldn't publish it. If the answer is no, then I would go ahead and write it.'"

By the time Dubus wrote this book, he was fifty years old. His father had died. The anger he'd felt toward his parents for a long time had dissipated. He'd forgiven them both. "I didn't even feel sorry for the boy I was, for the childhood I'd had." He wasn't trying to settle a score. "But I did feel artistically compelled to capture it, to paint it," he explains. "As artistically compelled to paint it as I would fiction." And Russo's words allowed him to do that.

"Do you have siblings?" he asks me then.

"Three brothers." I smile and add, "I already hear them saying to me . . ."

"'Ah, it wasn't like that, Melanie,'" he interrupts, his voice mimicking scorn.

"Exactly."

"Well, here's what you need to understand: your brothers are going to have their own stories to tell. You don't have to tell the *family* story. You have to tell *your* story of being in that family."

Dubus's strategy was to only write about his family in so far as their experience overlapped directly with his own. To illustrate, he describes writing about a particularly disturbing relationship his brother had with one of his middle school teachers. "If I'm walking by my brother's bedroom door at four o'clock on a Thursday afternoon in February, and I hear the sexual moaning of that Special Ed. teacher in there, I'm going to put in the moans. Because in the hallway, that's my memoir. But I'm not going to go on the other side of that door, because that's his." He holds up his hands. "How can I write honestly about my life as a fifteen-year-old boy without putting in the fact that nobody was doing anything about this grown woman practically living in our house in the afternoons, and I couldn't keep my little brother from wanting to die? How can I just cut that out of my story?" Taking that approach when handling any scenes that involved his siblings or his parents enabled Dubus to write a much more honest treatment of his memory of that time in his life.

Dubus is quick to add that when we venture into the process of writing memoir, it's also essential that we understand the difference between fact and truth. "The nature of truth is that it's largely subjective." In memoir, emotional truth can often diverge from the bare facts of what actually happened. He illustrates with a quick anecdote about a time when he heard a cousin of his say to her sisters that their father, a man who worked hundred-hour weeks and was rarely home, had never loved them. "She's factually totally wrong that their father did not love them," he says, musing that there was no way their father was working hundred-hour weeks for himself. "Yet, my cousin never saw him at breakfast, never saw him at lunch, never saw him at dinner, never saw him at bedtime, never saw him at a game, never saw him at a recital. So, her emotional truth is that she did not feel loved." The voices of doubt in our heads sometimes make us second-guess our own experiences, trying to sabotage our processes, but, according to Dubus, it's important that we honor our memories.

"We can't make shit up," Dubus qualifies, explaining that he's not at all promoting intentional fabrication. "We are allowed a small degree of poetic license," he says. There's a pivotal scene in his memoir where he's standing staring at his fourteen-year-old self in the mirror after watching his younger brother get beat up, and he vows to never walk away from a fight again. "I still see every bit of that afternoon, and I see it in a gray, April light." His brow creases into a frown. "But, you know, maybe there's a way now with Google Weather to go back forty years and actually look at what the weather was on April something 1973. And what if I discover it was a sunny day with blue sky? I don't care. I still see a gray sky, and I'm not changing that." He returns to the Tobias Wolff line: "'Memory has its own story to tell.' Trust your memory."

For Dubus, *Townie* is the result of approaching each part of his story with the rigorous curiosity that would open the panels of his memory and, then, trusting those memories. He writes in *the River Teeth* essay, "I had gone into my house and revealed whatever I felt it was important to reveal."

Dubus believes that we all have what he calls "a defined narrative arc." "They say when you're dying, you see your whole life. I think when you're writing, you start to see your whole life. I was surprised at what a defined narrative arc I had in my own life story so far. My memoir is a piece of my life story, mainly about being a boy and a young man. But I was a bullied kid who snapped and changed himself from passive to active, from being a victim to a predator, became very dangerous, discovered creative writing, and got onto the path of peace." He chuckles. "It sounds like an *Oprah* episode when you put it that way. But that is my story. It is what happened. And by writing it, I found the narrative arc."

"What did it feel like when you were finished?" I manage to sneak in this essential question.

"It felt really good." His shoulders relax. "I felt cleansed. If you look at the verb *express*—you know when you express a wound, you are actually squeezing the pus out; it's kind of a gross image—but when you express, you take what's in and you bring it out. And that can only be freeing, but you've got to get it all out. So you've got to be really true."

Expressing his truth through memoir connected Dubus to his readers in ways he wasn't normally accustomed to as a writer of fiction. Over and over again, people responded to his writing by thanking him for telling their story. Others expressed anger that he'd misrepresented their lives in some way. Still others responded with disappointment that his father, the author they'd revered, had largely failed at fatherhood. People staked their own claims to his story. It was confusing and frightening for Dubus to see himself and his story boxed in by other people's impressions. Yet, he's also realized that in writing nonfiction, that's exactly what happens. "Making your story public does relinquish ownership of it. But memoir is also just a moment in time." Dubus emphasizes that there's always room to grow and change as we take that moment and weave it into the moments yet to come. "This book doesn't even deal with the best years of my life, which is being a father and a husband."

Dubus's tone becomes more reflective. "I'm not one of these writers who ever feels really good about what I've written. I'm always haunted by what it's not. But with this one," he points to my copy of *Townie*, "I really felt like I went to the bottom of that experience at least with the subjective lens of my own memory."

"It still haunts me, though," he adds.

In a little while, I will sit and listen to a question–and–answer period after his public reading, and a question from a woman in the audience will prompt Dubus to reiterate this point about being haunted by the memories of his past. She will ask him if writing the memoir made him put this experience behind him. "The past is not the past," he'll say. "We all bring every second of our lives to who we are today."

What he reveals to me, though, as we wrap up our conversation, is this: "My new book, *Dirty Love*, which is the first one I've written after this, well, every piece of fiction I wrote before *Townie* had physical violence in it. *Dirty Love* is the first book that has no physical violence in it. It's almost as if by writing directly about it, I could move into other areas of human experience. It kind of freed me."

I inhale when he says this. Later, when I listen back to the recording of our conversation, I hear this intake of air. I'm breathing in his words, willing his outcome to oxygenate my own budding conviction to keep on going.

CHAPTER 2

Sue William Silverman

· *Because I Remember Terror, Father,*
I Remember You

· *Love Sick: One Woman's Journey*
Through Sexual Addiction

Author Sue William Silverman's first memoir, *Because I Remember Terror, Father, I Remember You,* is not an easy book to read. In a style that is both explicitly raw and profoundly vulnerable, she exposes the fourteen years of savage sexual abuse she suffered at the hands of her father while her mother remained silent and, therefore, complicit.

As I read these intertwined snapshots of memory that lay bare her fear, her pain, her confusion, her shame, her excruciating loneliness, I wept for this lost little girl. Sometimes, I felt bile rise at the back of my throat and rage surge through my veins. Most of all, I yearned to enter the pages and somehow rescue her. Get her out of that awful house filled with terror and violence, wrap her in my arms, and take her somewhere safe.

I recognize, though, that this memoir's very existence is comforting proof that Silverman doesn't need me to rescue her. She is already safe. How else could she have spoken the unspeakable

with such astounding artistry and grace? Without really knowing her, I am certain that, though the powerless, victimized
girl will probably always dwell somewhere inside of her, the
woman Silverman has become is a resilient and extraordinarily
courageous survivor.

I can also make this claim because I've met her once before
and had the privilege of hearing her speak. At the same 2013
Association of Writers and Writing Programs conference in Boston where Kim Stafford's words prompted this quest, I listened
to Silverman eloquently contradict some of the literary purists
who dismiss the idea that therapy and writing can have points of
intersection. Silverman is a brilliant writer, but she's also a gifted
and articulate speaker, able to fully engage with the room and
command our attention.

In a panel discussion called "This Is Not a Cigar: The Uses
of Therapy in a Writing Workshop," Silverman shared the
importance of involving selective therapeutic practices in the
writing-workshop setting—particularly when teaching students
of creative nonfiction. "Writing teachers are on the front lines of
emotional truth," she says. "Listening and safety are two of the
most valuable things I learned from my therapist. Our students
need to feel like they are in a safe place where their voices can be
heard and valued before any issues of craft can be raised."

Silverman is speaking from a vast reserve of experience. She's
taught prose in the low-residency MFA program at the Vermont
College of Fine Arts since 2003 and led countless prose workshops.

After the panel, a writer friend, a recent VCFA graduate, introduced me to Silverman. A petite woman with strawberry-blonde
hair, Silverman is bubbly and down to earth. In that first brief
interaction, I sensed a profound kindness in her. So, when I start
considering the writers whose memoirs have been particularly
meaningful to me and whose journeys to tell their hard stories I
want to unpack, Sue William Silverman tops my list.

She responds to my pitch less than three hours after I e-mail
her, writing, "Thank you for letting me know what my work has

meant to you. I'm truly touched. It also means a lot to me to know some of your own story. And it's a powerful one. I think that's so very important that you moved to a place where you could discover *your* story within the story of your family. That shows much courage, and I admire you."

Admiration coming from an author like Sue William Silverman is no little thing. *Because I Remember Terror, Father, I Remember You* won the Association of Writers and Writing Programs Award for Creative Nonfiction in 1995. Since then, she's written two more memoirs. *Love Sick: One Woman's Journey Through Sexual Addiction*, written in a bold and lyrical style, recounts Silverman's years of destructive sexual behavior and how she traveled the difficult road to recovery and self-value. The memoir was made into a Lifetime Original Movie in 2008. Her latest book, *The Pat Boone Fan Club: My Life as a White Anglo-Saxon Jew*, released just a week before I e-mailed her, is a sometimes funny, often tender account of her fascination with the pop music icon and his public image as a loving and safe father, juxtaposed against the brutality of her own father. It's a story of finding a place to belong. Silverman has also published a collection of poems, *Hieroglyphics in Neon*, and her guidebook for writers venturing to tell their personal stories, *Fearless Confessions: A Writer's Guide to Memoir*, has been positioned alongside Anne Lamott's *Bird by Bird*, Natalie Goldberg's *Writing Down the Bones*, and Stephen King's *On Writing* as an essential reading and teaching text that addresses the craft and psychological challenge of memoir writing.

By breaking the silence that so often shadows the topics of incest and sex addiction, Silverman has become a sought-after speaker and advocate for victims of abuse. She's appeared on numerous radio and television shows, including *The View* and *Anderson Cooper 360*, and has been the subject of a Discovery Channel documentary and a John Stossel ABC-TV special. "Your voice is out there," she tells me from her home office in Michigan when we meet via Skype on a Friday afternoon in March. Though she's nine hundred miles away, the wonders of technology give us the chance to talk face-to-face, with only a screen between us. "You start playing a different role. Now you are the expert."

She chuckles as she continues, "If you went into a bookstore and asked for *Because I Remember Terror, Father, I Remember You*, it would be in the child-abuse section. It's not going to be in some sort of literary section." She laughs because she used to balk at this pigeonholing of her work. "And then I had to say, 'Get over yourself. What difference does it make?' Yes, I see myself as a literary writer, but my books really have helped people."

When she started writing about her childhood, Silverman did not set out to gain recognition as a survivor of abuse. "I sat down to write," she says, "and what became *Terror*, fell out of me, like in three months. Page after page just came rolling out of the printer. Clearly I had something to say about myself."

Silverman describes her process. "I wrote in a brain fever. It really almost came out of the ether, you could say, except on some deeper level, I think that thought [of writing my story] had been with me for a long, long time."

And for a long, long time, Silverman kept that thought hidden, even from herself. Like so many other memoirists who trained as fiction writers, she spent ten years writing the book as a novel. In the 1980s, when she started writing, Silverman says, "I'd never even heard the word 'memoir.' No one was writing one. You were a poet or you were a fiction writer or a journalist. So I saw myself as a novelist. And I did not have the slightest thought of writing memoir. I'd never even read one, outside of maybe *The Diary of Anne Frank*. Other than that, nothing."

She wrote six novels that were all in some way about incest. "But I sort of was wearing a mask," she admits, "because I certainly wasn't going to admit to it myself." Silverman kept up the charade that the characters in her novels were in no way connected to her. "I mean, when I think back on it now, one of those novels is even about sex addiction before the term 'sex addiction' was even around. It's so weird that I was writing about myself having no idea that I was writing about myself. And if somebody had asked me then if I was writing about myself, I would have said, 'No, of course not.'"

In her books and when she speaks, Silverman is candid about how therapy played a central role in helping her cope with and sort through her trauma. She says it was her therapist, and not another writer, who suggested that she might want to write her story as a memoir, a true story. "At that point," she says, laughing, "I thought that he was the crazy person, not me!" She couldn't see herself as someone worth writing about. "How I saw myself was as this pathetic person who couldn't do anything. I was just a loser and a failure." She laughs again and adds, "You know, all of those nice messages we speak to ourselves." It appears that many of us on the journey to tell our stories are experts in self-sabotage.

Silverman continued to resist the idea of telling her real story. And then, within days of each other, both of her parents died, and her therapist said, "Sue, maybe now you'll feel safe enough to write about yourself."

To humor him, she thought she'd maybe write a short essay. "Then it was just so there, that I couldn't stop writing," she says. "I didn't question or think of anything. The words were just there. The images were just there. The metaphors were just there."

Silverman kept the writing very close, though, and didn't share it with anyone in process, not even her therapist. "I didn't want anybody influencing what I had to say. I didn't show it to my sister, and say, 'Are you okay with this?' Because it doesn't matter if she's okay with it or not. Yes, it would be nice if she's okay with it, but if she's not okay with it, I'm still going to write it. I own my story. If she disagrees with it, then she gets to write her own book if she wants. This is what happened to me. This is my truth. This was my story, and I needed to tell it."

The point that Silverman emphasizes for me, though, is that the ease with which the story came to her, and her ability to own it, would not have happened without those ten years of writing fiction. "Even though it's fiction, let's face it, you're still learning how to write. I was learning how to do dialogue; I was learning how to construct a plot or arc; I was learning how to develop a character on the page. It was just that with the memoir, it just so happened that character was me."

Silverman had learned the craft of writing, so when she was finally ready to write this story, she didn't really have to think about craft at all. And the story rolled out of her so quickly, she says that there was no time for it to frighten her.

"Writing *Love Sick* was much scarier," she says, than writing *Terror* and reassures me that although her first experience was different, fear in the memoir-writing process is completely natural.

"With *Terror*," she explains, "you know you're writing about yourself as a little kid, and this adult, this father, is doing something to you. That has a sort of a built-in sympathy for you."

Silverman did not feel that same cover of safety with *Love Sick* because the choices she recounts in that book are her own. "Writing about being a sex addict is like: Here I am; I'm an adult. I am having affairs with married men when I myself am married. I'm cheating on my husband. I'm doing all of this really bad behavior and destructive behavior. So, what are people going to think of me?"

Silverman tries to ignore those thoughts about other people's reactions and keep her focus on the writing, something she also encourages her students to do. But, when she was writing *Love Sick*, she had a hard time looking at herself on the page and knowing she'd done those things. And even though she says she had good reason for her behavior—"Basically, my father told me I was just good for sex and that was it"—Silverman had so much shame that she says she sometimes did question whether to write her story.

I ask Silverman if she encountered any of the same stumbling blocks with *Terror*, even though the writing of that first memoir was so intense that perhaps she didn't really have time to question things.

"The interesting thing about the first book, the two sections that I had the most trouble writing—and probably you'll find this sort of ironic, because I do—were not about the child abuse, not about what my father had done to me. The two sections that just brought me to my knees were the sections where my parents died and where my cat died." The pain that crosses Silverman's features highlights the grief in those memories. She confides, "I just was a basket case, and I would have to lie down and just sob for a while."

The reason for those powerful reactions, Silverman believes, is because those two events were much more recent. She'd sorted out a lot of the childhood experiences in therapy, but her parents' deaths happened about two weeks before she started writing, and her beloved cat, the one thing she felt responsible for in her life, had just died, as well. "I hadn't really processed that in any other way significantly, say in therapy, so I would never, if I went out to give a reading, even now, I would never read either of those sections." I hear a tremor in her voice.

"How were you able to keep writing them?" I ask.

"I knew that they had to be part of the story," she replies. "Those two events, those deaths were so big and significant that they just . . . I knew that they had to be in this book. But I don't think I could even look at those sections today without crying. It was just so tough."

In *Terror*, Silverman writes about the difficult truths that her parents' deaths revealed to her: "My father and my mother each had a choice, could have chosen a different definition of love. They could have realized they didn't know how to love their children healthy, love them well. [. . .] They were the parents, the adults, they chose to be. We all are the parents, the adults, we choose to be."

These insights only came to Silverman by writing through those scenes. "The reason why I write memoir," she says now, "is to be able to see the experience itself in a way. I hardly know what I think until I write. The therapy is one way of sort of processing things. But it's only in writing about some of these things that we discover and understand the metaphors of our experience that give our life meaning. Writing is a way to organize your life, give it a frame, give it a structure, so that you can really see what it was that happened."

"When you'd framed your experience into *Terror*, when you'd finished, how did it feel?"

"It felt really good, actually. I felt relieved. It was very different than when I finished writing the novels, because on some level I knew the novels were all really awful and that they really were never going to get published. I could tell the difference. I knew the book was worthy of publication. I knew my genre was creative nonfiction. I had found my voice."

And finding her voice and speaking her experience shifted how Silverman viewed the genre, a shift that reaffirms Kim Stafford's feelings when he received the galley of his memoir. Silverman says, "I could hold this book, this tangible thing. And it takes it out of you. It's like writing that pressure out of the pressure cooker. Each word that comes out is like taking a little piece of pain with it and putting it on the page. Which isn't to say that you don't still have feelings about it. Of course you do. But it just takes away a lot of that power it has over you, and you feel a kind of distance towards it. Now when I think about my father and incest, I think about, okay, now wait, what page is that on?"

She twists around in her desk chair and gestures behind her to the open-backed shelves stacked with books. "It's like, yeah I remember it in the real world, but it's more like: it's over there. It's in the bookcase."

There's so much beauty in Silverman's metaphor. Her story is something she looks at on her terms. Something she can choose to take off the shelf. And something she can always choose to put back.

Those books on Silverman's bookshelf have had a profound impact on the people who've read them. An impact that Silverman did not anticipate. "I really had no idea what to expect. I thought I would get a few literary reviews, give a few readings, and call it a day."

Instead, after writing *Because I Remember Terror, Father, I Remember You*, she was inundated with letters, hundreds of them, from people, mainly women, thanking her for giving voice to their experiences. "They feel that because they don't have that voice and they don't write, my book comforts them, which I find so sweet and empowering and endearing. They can say, 'Thank you for telling your story because I feel that my story is also out there.'"

The media response to *Love Sick* was slightly different. Silverman admits to a few uncomfortable radio interviews where, instead of sympathizing with her addiction, "shock jocks" asked her some markedly humiliating questions about her sex life. But overall, *Love Sick* produced similar responses to those she'd had with *Terror*. "I'll get e-mails from people who say, 'Oh my God, I had no idea why I was having these affairs or doing this stuff, but because of your book, I realize I've got the same problem that you have.'" Silverman's story gives these people hope that they can find a path to recovery through therapy, too. She says those sorts of responses far outweigh the indignity she experienced with a few interview questions asked in poor taste. "The important thing, and what you have to keep your eye on, is the fact that you can write a book that touches people." She pauses, then, her face breaking into a brilliant smile, she exclaims, "Can you ask for more as a writer? That's just so moving."

With what I recognize as characteristic humility, Silverman says, "Growing up, I was just this pathetic little kid. I got terrible grades. I got the worst SAT scores in the history of the universe. I never studied. I didn't know who I was. I was just limping through life. So I often ask myself, How did this happen? How did I even get a teaching job? It's just all amazing, and I would not have anticipated any of it."

She goes on to say that she never would have expected, almost twenty years after the publication of *Terror*, someone like me to both be reading it and asking about it. "Even though your background isn't mine and mine isn't yours, there's so much common ground from those universal emotions and feelings—alienation, loss, grief." Silverman's compassion and generosity of spirit is so clear. "It's an honor that people want to tell me their stories, too, and that they trust me enough to do so."

Writing her memoirs and recognizing that people will place her in unforeseen roles, such as spokesperson or advocate, have given Silverman an important understanding about how readers see her and how she sees herself: "I've let any worry about [people's expectations] go. Every book is me, but not the whole me." Incest and sex addiction are not the only defining factors to her personhood. Writing about those slices of her life has cleared the way for her to see other slices of herself, too, and she continues to write about them. She alludes to a fourth memoir in the works, what she describes as "a story I'm still trying to find my way through" that explores, among other things, getting older and her bizarre fear of dying. "I feel confident now that it's going to find its way," she says. "That it's going to be a cohesive something."

Silverman the writing teacher now enters our discussion. "You will find more stories, too, because there is more to you than just this one thing," she assures me. "In some ways you can't see it yet, which is good because you do need to focus on what you need to focus on now. And then more stories will come."

Our conversation is drawing to a close, and I'm down to my last question. "Is there anything else you'd like me to know that I haven't thought to ask?"

In her answer, I'm anticipating maybe more discussion about her latest stories, more information about her newest memoir. But instead, Silverman leans closer, her sweet face filling my laptop screen, her brown eyes full of light, and she says, "I want you to know that you can do it. You can."

My eyes fill with unexpected tears.

"It is lonely and it's hard to be a writer," Silverman continues, seeing the rawness of my emotion. "You have to know that you are the same as me. I'm the same as you. It doesn't matter that I've published a book or not. It doesn't matter. We're all writers. We are all in this together. We help each other. We lift each other.

You know, I will be thinking about you a lot and cheering you on," she says, and I am again so struck by her kindness. "What you are doing is really important. You can do this. You are not alone. You will do this."

I love these generous words. Words from a wise and compassionate writer who deeply understands how hard it is to travel the lonely road of writing a hard story. Their sincerity washes over me. I feel a tiny sprout of confidence poking through my doubts, and in that briefest of moments, I believe her.

CHAPTER 3

Michael Patrick MacDonald

· All Souls: A Family Story from Southie

It takes a few moments for the angry shouts to penetrate our conversation, but when the string of profanities mounts in volume and intensity, author and activist Michael Patrick MacDonald and I both turn our gazes to the busy street adjacent to where we sit conversing on a patio in Roxbury's Dudley Square just in time to see a woman wildly swing what looks like the handle of a broom or shovel at another woman standing a few feet away from her.

"Oh, my God," MacDonald says, rising from his seat. "Has she got a weapon?" He starts walking toward them. "Call 911," he says to me over his shoulder.

I pick up my cell and dial, describing to the operator the three women on the street—two white, one African American—all in their mid-twenties, and the escalating screaming match, punctuated by violent swipes from the broomstick. As I'm talking, two of the women cross to the other side of Washington Street, while the woman with the broom handle continues her rant, her shrill voice trailing them as they move further away.

Several pedestrians walk around the woman and her tirade, averting their eyes, but MacDonald stands at the driveway entrance to the parking lot, his hands tucked into the front pockets of his jeans, husky shoulders slightly bent, his demeanor calm, directing words I can't hear to the woman with the broom. After a few more minutes, the woman turns away and trudges down the street out of sight, just as a patrol car pulls in next to MacDonald. He exchanges a few words with the officer and then saunters back to our table.

"That's like Southie," he says matter-of-factly when he sits back down. "She's on heroin, which is always obvious to me, and she knows the other woman from jail." He chuckles. "I didn't want to get hit with the broom, but I was trying to get her to stop instigating it. 'Let her go,' I told her. 'Let her go.'" His voice softens and concern wrinkles his broad forehead. "She's really messed up."

"When you step back into those kinds of situations, does it feel jarring to you?" I ask.

"I feel like it follows me," MacDonald says with a sigh, and his blue eyes reveal the intensity of his own lived experience. "That world follows me all the time."

"That world" was MacDonald's daily existence growing up during the 1970s and '80s in South Boston's Old Colony housing project, when the area claimed the highest concentration of white poverty in America. "That world," riddled with violence, addiction, and crime and touting a proud code of silence, also claimed the lives of four of MacDonald's brothers. And "that world," of which MacDonald writes, "We were proud to be from here, as proud as we were to be Irish," is as much a character as the characters themselves in his piercing memoir *All Souls: A Family Story from Southie*. A national best seller and winner of an American Book Award in 2000, *All Souls* portrays the overlapping light and darkness in the tight-knit, Irish-Catholic Southie community during an era of gangster violence led by notorious crime boss James "Whitey" Bulger. On page after page, MacDonald chronicles how his family was rocked by violence and loss in an insular culture of abject poverty and gangs and drugs.

In writing *All Souls*, MacDonald also gives voice to the unspoken trauma and despair experienced by countless other families from the neighborhood. On this early October day, MacDonald has chosen the Haley House Bakery and Café in Boston's Roxbury neighborhood as the location for our interview. The bakery, one branch of a larger nonprofit organization committed to community development and restoration, including after-school programs and transitional employment for ex-offenders, is a charming space that regularly showcases the work of local artists. For privacy and because the fall chill hadn't quite arrived yet, we'd decided, after getting warm drinks, to sit outside on the raised patio at an orange plastic picnic table. It seems a fitting location for me to get to know this man who has transformed his personal ordeal into community activism and a passion for social justice.

"It's cool that we ended up in Roxbury," MacDonald tells me when we first sit down. "So much of my story is here; that's where I really got my voice."

He's referring to his discovery of community organizing in 1990 and how his involvement with a group called Citizens for Safety, working in Roxbury and the Dorchester neighborhood, finally gave him a safe space to tell his story. "Through community organizing I discovered a place to put it all, to transform all that pain into something useful in the world, into something meaningful, into a reason to be here, to not kill myself or do drugs or get messed up—disappear myself in whatever way. It was in community organizing that I found a purpose for the story long before I put it in a book." MacDonald's second memoir, *Easter Rising*, is an in-depth chronicle of this personal reinvention.

By the time he began work in community organizing, Mac-Donald had lived through the deaths of three of his older brothers in a six-year time span and the near death of his older sister. His brother Davey jumped off the roof of their housing complex. His brother Frankie was killed in a botched bank robbery. His brother Kevin was found hanged in prison under suspicious circumstances. His sister Kathy fell off the roof of their building and suffered irreversible brain damage. Another brother, Patrick, had died in infancy before MacDonald was born. Then, in 1990, his fourteen-year-old brother, Stevie, was falsely accused of murder and railroaded by the police after finding his best friend bleeding from a gunshot wound.

MacDonald says that the injustices around Stevie's case were the triggers that helped him to start seeing the broader injustices in both his family history and his community history—injustices around race and class and crime that nobody was talking about. It was then, he explains, that the idea of writing a book began to formulate in his mind.

"But I didn't write a book," he says. "I didn't start writing until seven years later, but what I did do is started turning all that experience into social action."

Part of the difficulty in following through on his book idea is that the words for his story were not words MacDonald had ever been able to access. "The words that I needed to say around violence, murder, drugs, pain killing, oppression, police violence—all those words that I needed to say, we couldn't say in my neighborhood because we had a code of silence. We had a gangster-imposed code of silence, so we couldn't say the words. It was actually dangerous. You could die. You could get killed for saying those words in relation to the neighborhood."

But, to his surprise, MacDonald found that there were people who were saying those words in other places. "I would see people on the evening news from this neighborhood," he says, gesturing toward the Roxbury streets surrounding us, "saying the words that we couldn't say. Mothers of murdered children, ministers, activists, street workers—they'd all appear on the television saying all these words that were relevant to my life—*violence, poverty, oppression, drugs, police brutality*—and that's when I knew I needed to come over here. That's when I crossed the bridge, a bridge that most people didn't cross out of Southie."

MacDonald is talking about the actual Broadway Bridge, which connects South Boston to downtown Boston, but he's also talking about a metaphorical bridge that crossed from his mainly white Southie to the overwhelmingly black neighborhoods of Roxbury and Dorchester, where he encountered African Americans with experiences that mirrored his own. "I brought my story with me and worked with other people who had a story, and we all collectively—and I didn't know this at the time, and I didn't have the language for what I'm talking about now—but what I feel like we were doing was working with our stories, bringing our stories together to kind of change the narrative."

With other community organizers, MacDonald ran gun buy-back programs and worked to establish community support groups with mothers of murdered children to provide space for others to tell their stories. "I'd be the one organizing the press conference," he explains, "then they'd slowly push me up there to tell my story because they knew why I was in this stuff, too, and I would tell a little bit about how my life was impacted." A smile breaks across MacDonald's face, transforming it entirely—resting, the intensity of his expression could easily be mistaken for anger. He took the "safe" route, the one that wouldn't get him in trouble when his words appeared in the newspaper the next day. "I wasn't saying that this was a systemic thing that we'd been dealing with in our neighborhood. I was taking it a little bit at a time."

Taking it a little bit at a time is the philosophy MacDonald uses with his own writing students. He is author-in-residence in Northeastern University's Honors Department and teaches memoir and social justice classes. He also conducts community workshops in trauma writing. "When a person tells the trauma story, they need to be in control of it every bit of the way—of how much they are going to tell, when they're going to tell it, where they're going to tell it. They're in charge. They don't have to share it with the world. They can write it and destroy it."

The process of beginning to tell his own story started to ease a burden MacDonald had been carrying for a long time. A burden that wasn't just an emotional weight but a physical one, too. "I called it 'heavy head'—that was the only way I could describe it. My head felt so heavy I could barely lift it." However, the more he talked about what he'd been through, the more he realized what that talking was doing for him. "I felt lighter," he explains.

After almost a decade of telling his story in this way, through his community-organizing work, MacDonald recognized that he needed to commit the words he'd been speaking to the page— not just for himself but for all of the people back in Southie who weren't telling their stories. "Nobody was dealing with white working-class and poor people, and I came to realize that that's where I needed to go. I started to be really conscious about what this is about and realized that I needed to go deeper. That's why I wrote the book."

"What was it like for you to start diving into those memories?" I ask.

"I was writing the book always. All my life. I'm visual. I drew pictures all my life. I have . . . that taking-pictures kind of memory. I filter. We all filter, but we pay attention to what matters. I have snapshots in my head, and I remember details, especially around trauma." MacDonald admits that accessing those details was not easy. He wasn't that far removed from the situations he'd endured to not still feel their effects. "I remember when I'd write hard stuff, I would throw up—I threw up a few times. But another response would be to just sleep for like a long, long, long time— like, go to sleep and wake up the next day. I was pacing the floors and smoking; I was smoking when I wrote the book, and I smoked a lot back then. So there were all kinds of responses."

As difficult as those responses were, the process of writing down his memories revealed things to MacDonald that he'd never understood before. "What we remember and how we remember it really tells us how we became who we became."

He cites a particular scene from *All Souls* when, during the infamous busing riots that broke out in Southie in 1974, he witnessed the brutal beating of a Haitian man after he'd been dragged from his car. "I didn't even know that was going to be in the book; I didn't know that it was an important story in my life until it kind of came out as a memory. And then, when it did come out, I realized why I remembered it with such detail. That story encapsulates a lot about who I am. It encapsulates my whole perspective on race and class." MacDonald goes on to explain that the memory wasn't just about seeing a black man being dragged from his car by white people. It was the shock of seeing a black man being dragged from a car by white people who were themselves so deprived. "I was only nine," he continues, "but snapshotting it the way I did at nine says an awful lot about my worldview on race and class. Not that it justifies the beating or excuses it, but I saw how these people who had nothing—they didn't have a pot to piss in—yet they found someone that they thought might be less than them. That whole race and class dynamic is everything to me in this country."

Figuring out *how* to tell the story in a way that might speak to that developing perspective didn't happen right away. "I'd write stuff and not write stuff or think about writing stuff or tell people I was writing a book because I got an advance—I'd written a proposal, but I didn't have writing done. So I was telling people I was writing a book, but I wasn't really writing a book." He laughs and says he doesn't think the people around him took him too seriously at first. "We live in that kind of place—well, Boston's that kind of place—where you have an idea about what you're going to do with your life and you walk into the bar and you tell people, 'I have this great idea!' And people are like, 'Yeah right, good luck.' Nobody takes any kind of big ideas or transformational things that seriously until you actually do them."

"Did you ever question whether you should write the book?" I ask.

"I honestly didn't know anybody would really read it beyond my friends in the nonprofit world, the activist world—people who were kind of 'safe.' I didn't know what it would become." That ignorance enabled MacDonald to explore the story without really considering the implications of how people might react to what he was saying.

MacDonald spent five or six months stutter-stepping around the story before hitting on the thing that would point him in the right direction. He picks up my copy of *All Souls* and opens to the first page of chapter 2 and begins reading: "'My oldest memories are of my mother crying.' I got that line from watching *Goodfellas*. The opening line of the movie is 'As far back as I can remember, I always wanted to be a gangster.' The simplicity of that sentence made me think: What's the furthest back thing I can remember?" And what MacDonald remembered was that story about seeing his mother crying over her baby, Patrick Michael, who died before MacDonald was born. "It is my oldest memory, and that story captures so much about the rest of the book, because the people I end up working with are also grieving mothers, whether they're from Roxbury, Dorchester, Mattapan—black, Latino, Asian—that becomes my life's work. And it was only writing that line that I realized, holy fuck, these are the people that matter most to me, and it starts with that scene about coming upon my mother."

MacDonald understood then that the story would be chronological, and in seeing the chronology, he saw the target he wanted to reach. "I knew where we were going: the vigil. The naming of names. All of the book was increasingly about the unspoken stuff. So I knew we were going there."

All Souls opens and closes with a vigil MacDonald organized in the Gate of Heaven Church in Southie on November 2, 1996, All Souls Night, where the names of 250 "lives lost too soon," including MacDonald's four brothers, Patrick, Davey, Frankie, and Kevin, were read aloud for the first time. "That first year, we thought maybe five or ten people would show up," MacDonald tells me. "But the church was packed, and people got up there and said the names of their loved ones, and I saw their faces change when they would light the candle and say the name, and it was transformative for me. Incredibly transformative. I learned even more what happens when you name the stuff and say the words. It was really the beginning of a truth-telling movement in Southie." So many of the hard truths MacDonald artfully renders in his memoir opened the door for that movement, too.

"When I knew it was going toward the vigil, I knew my family's deaths were part of a much bigger bloodbath. A much bigger atrocity. It's the same as with your father and all the people who died of AIDS. It's like a holocaust. It's unbelievable. But when you know that, you kind of have a better sense of the bigger picture, why this matters to everyone else."

I think about the scenes in the book that resonated with the same intensity of grief as some of my experiences, the ones that stayed with me long after putting the book down: the image of Davey lying in the street, the family sitting day after day at Kathy's bedside hoping she'd awaken from her coma, the story of Frankie's death and how he could have been saved. "What were the hardest things for you to write about?" I ask MacDonald.

He admits that if I'd asked him this question a few years ago, he probably wouldn't have been able to answer it. "I just went through it in a kind of numb way." Two years ago, though, he was asked to read the whole book for audio, and there were a number of times where he had to stop and take a break because he started crying. "For fifteen years, I've been doing talks and readings from this book, but I've been selective in what I'm reading. Hard stuff. Stuff that hits the audience hard, but not stuff where it's going to make me break down. The trauma story, it's old. It's kind of boring to me, to be honest."

I'd heard these exact same words from some of the other writers I'd talked to, this idea that the telling of the story becomes so commonplace that it loses the emotional weight it once carried. MacDonald says, "I thought reading the audiobook would just be nothing. But the parts where I would break down or we would have to stop, take a break, go to dinner, come back, and try again—even in the audio you can hear me choking up a few times, because later I said, 'You know what? Keep that.' But the passages that I discovered were hardest were nothing around my grief at all, but anytime I'm reporting on someone telling someone else that someone's dead—if I had to read publicly when Johnnie knocks on the door and my mother opens it . . ." MacDonald's voice cracks, and he swipes his hand over his eyes. I feel the emotion filling the pause in the sentence. "I can't even say it now. I'm having a hard time saying it now." He stops again and pulls in a breath. "Her telling him that Davey died. It's weird because that's not poor me; that's poor him and poor her. Other people's pain is so much harder. I can't even think about it. But it's about those people and not me."

That those memories still affected him deeply actually made MacDonald happy. "I don't want to say that it's just, you know, boring. You want to make sure that you can still feel." The audiobook experience reminded him that he still did.

I pick up *All Souls* and hold it out in front of us. "So what did it feel like when you were finished and actually had this to hold?"

"I felt like a new person," MacDonald answers immediately. "I went into writing this as a person who was staying alive by doing emergency work. All that work I was involved in was keeping me in the world with some meaning and purpose, but I can't say that I really loved being alive." He qualifies, "I wasn't suicidal, but I didn't love life." He rests his hand on the book. "When I finished and it was a book, I really, really loved being alive. I hadn't remembered what that was like."

But then, he tells me, the book went public, and it turned out it wasn't only friends who read it. "And I was like: Fuck, what did I do? There were people who wanted to kill me and other people were thinking I'd betrayed them."

When MacDonald says people wanted to kill him, he's not exaggerating. Exposing his truth exposed a lot about the neighborhood he came from. And, early on, not everyone was happy about it. MacDonald received death threats. He had to cancel an appearance at the South Boston branch of the Boston Public Library because someone tipped him off that there were protestors who planned to attack him. One day, a car full of guys from Southie followed him for blocks and he had to hide out for a while. Most of the threats came from people from the neighborhood who hadn't even read the book but had heard rumors about what was in it. People were afraid MacDonald was telling *their* secrets, even though most of the "secrets" were common knowledge. "They were all living in this fantasy that nobody knew."

He tells me about the time a neighbor showed up at his door demanding to know what he'd written about her family. He reminds me of the scene in *All Souls* when this neighbor's father stabbed her two brothers and MacDonald's mother basically saved their lives. "She said, 'What's in there about the fucking rape?' and I didn't know anything about a rape. I only told stories that are my stories. Of course, they involve other people, and that's the problem, but I only told parts of their stories if they intersected with my trauma."

There were many responses to his book like this one. "People would come up to me and say, 'You wrote that book.' And I didn't know whether they wanted to kill me or cry with me."

The people who wanted to cry with him far outnumbered the people who were angry, though. And to MacDonald, that made publishing the book worthwhile, no matter what the repercussions. "I was afraid for my life for a minute, but so many people were thanking me, and that held me steady. 'Thank you for telling the truth about the neighborhood,' they'd say. Or, 'This book saved my life.' It's so worth it to be doing it."

"Was your family's reaction to the story any different?" I ask.

"My mother still hasn't read it," he answers. "But she's heard what's in it. It was on the radio and television, so she'll often hear from people what's in it, and she's fine with it. I left it up to my siblings if they wanted to read it." He's quick to add, "But I would never force people to read another person's telling of traumas that they lived. It's up to them. We all have our processes that get us to this point where we are able to tell the story. That doesn't mean everyone else who's lived an aspect of that story is able to go there. Or read it."

Leaning forward, his elbows pressed into the picnic table, MacDonald emphasizes an important lesson that I've heard before but need to continue to hear. "They don't get to have an opinion on me telling my story. That's the truth. I didn't tell their story. I told my story." Earlier in our conversation, I'd expressed some of my fears about telling my own story. I know MacDonald is speaking directly to those fears when he says, "If you're going to live in this world, survive in this world, in a healthy way and be okay with being in this world, you just have to do this. You just have to do it, and it has to be the priority. But how much you then want to share is completely up to you. This process, the cathartic process, to use the cliché that we all hear, is like none other."

MacDonald never dreamed that fifteen years after its publication, *All Souls* would still be making an impact. "Thirteen-, fourteen-year-olds who weren't even born when I wrote it are hooked on it. Kids who don't look like me, necessarily, but people from different classes, people from different races, are still reading it and relating to it, even though it's about the '70s and '80s. There's no reference to anything they know now. No smartphones—I'm describing things like turning the dial on the TV to change the channel! Yet they're still telling me they related to it."

In a few weeks' time, I'll bear witness to this phenomenon when I sit in an auditorium on Northeastern University's campus that's packed with high school students from all over the city who have come, with copies of *All Souls* clutched in their hands, to hear MacDonald read and talk about social justice and truth-telling. Afterwards, they'll stand in long lines, while MacDonald signs their books and engages in conversation way past the "official" end to the evening.

"When you really go there with your own truths," he says, "you end up in a universal place. This is what happens, and it's fucking magic. It's about something bigger than you. It's beyond you. All the stuff that still happens in this world with this book isn't about me. But I was a conduit. I feel like I was a conduit for a story that needed to be told."

We have to wrap up our conversation because MacDonald is attending a fund-raising event in Dorchester, "Men of Boston Cook for Women's Health," where he's participating as a "celebrity chef" along with Massachusetts governor Charlie Baker, Boston mayor Marty Walsh, Massachusetts congressman Michael Capuano, CNN's John King, former New England Patriots players Patrick Pass and Jermaine Wiggins, and an impressive list of other local celebrities and nonprofit and business leaders in the community. I offer to drive him.

In the car, as we weave through rush-hour traffic on the streets of Roxbury and Dorchester, MacDonald points to different landmarks in the area that he remembers from his childhood. Most of his sentences begin with the words, "That used to be . . ." Over the past twenty years, these areas have seen significant changes through real estate development and an influx of new businesses—a gentrification that has dramatically altered the social infrastructure that once existed. Million-dollar, luxury condos are even now replacing the church where MacDonald watched as pallbearers carried the caskets of his three brothers down the steps.

"It's like a whole different population walking on the street a lot of the times. It's two extremes, really. The old-school crowd is like those girls fighting on the street earlier today, more junked out than ever, and then there's the people taking their dogs to doggie day care." I hear the wistful tone in MacDonald's voice when he says, "So much is gone."

There's no doubt that MacDonald deeply loves this place, despite all the pain and trauma he endured there. Even with all the bad stuff that happened, he says he wouldn't change it for

the world. Everything he knows about community and connect-
edness he got from living in the Old Colony project and its surrounding neighborhood. "And that's why I'm so happy I wrote
the book. It's not true what they say about how you can't go home
again. When you write memoir, you can. When this is all gone,"
he waves his hands at the familiar but not familiar streets of the
old neighborhood, "I'll always be able to go home."

CHAPTER 4

Joan Wickersham

· *The Suicide Index: Putting My
Father's Death in Order*

I meet Joan Wickersham at Dado Tea in Cambridge, Massachusetts. The café is a modish space with clean lines and walls adorned with Asian decor. Bright light streams in through the floor-to-ceiling windows at the front of the shop. On this frosty Monday morning in March 2014, the place is quiet. It's not hard to identify Wickersham as the elegant woman sipping tea in front of a laptop at a small wooden table in the back corner. The only other patron in the shop is obviously a student, whose computer, books, and papers clutter her table. This is the sort of place where I'd choose to camp out with my work, too.

Wickersham stands as I approach and welcomes me with a gracious smile. She's in her late fifties, her dark hair cut in a smart bob. A silky, rose-colored scarf wraps in loose folds around her neck. I'm drawn to her warmth and grace, and after getting a steaming cup of tea for myself, I settle into the seat across from her for our conversation and feel quite like I'm about to have a chat with an old friend.

As contradictory as this sounds, when I read Wickersham's memoir, *The Suicide Index: Putting My Father's Death in Order*, the ache that often resides in my chest simultaneously intensified and diminished. The intensity emerged from a place of understanding. I don't claim to understand Wickersham's unique experience. My father did not kill himself, as Wickersham's did. But I do understand aspects of her grief: Her confusion. Her obsessive need to make sense of something so nonsensical. To tell his story and hers in some way. There's a strand of universal experience that binds her story to mine. And the poignant communion that happens when someone else's pain mirrors our own, when someone else's words could be our words, made my chest ache.

At the same time, the ache diminished when I discovered Wickersham's approach to her story: its unconventional, nonlinear frame that takes the form of an index with headings like *act of, anger about, finding some humor in, other people's stories concerning, psychological impact of.* Her book holds promise that there are unique ways to tell complicated stories and do them the justice they deserve. To any of us who keep peeling back what seem like endless layers of our stories, feeling their complexity, and questioning how we'll ever find a way to really tell them, Wickersham's work is deeply reassuring. "That's so much more what one struggles with in writing a personal story. It is how to craft it, but it's not how to craft it in terms of making it polished. It's how to craft it in a way that is true to the experience," Wickersham reflects as we delve into the intricacies of how her memoir came to be.

The path to her memoir's creation was, for Wickersham, in some ways just as complex and chaotic as living through the aftermath of her father's suicide. Writing the book was an eleven-year process. Wickersham was thirty-three when her father killed himself in 1991. She wrote the first piece connected to his death in 1995. She completed *The Suicide Index* in 2006.

"What made you decide to start writing about your father?" I ask, warming my hands on my teacup.

"I think I just knew," Wickersham tells me. "I was a writer, and then this big thing happened in my family. And the way that I tend to try to understand things is through stories—both things that I write and things that I read. That's the deepest way I know of expressing something inexpressible. I knew that this was a big thing and I didn't understand it, and I wanted to understand it. It felt like there was a story there, and I felt like I wanted to get at it."

A fiction writer first, Wickersham's natural instinct, like Sue Silverman's, was to try to tell this story in novel form. "I worked on it as a novel for about eight years," she says. "I used all the writer's tricks. I did it as a third-person chronological novel. I did it as a third-person chronological novel with flashbacks. I did it as a first-person novel. I just thought, If I could only find the right way to tell this story in this novel, then it would somehow unlock the whole thing. And I just couldn't get it."

In the spring of 2003, she had a completed draft of the novel, but it fell flat. Her agent couldn't sell it. "I was devastated," Wickersham recalls. "I felt like this was the 'big story.' Here I am a writer, this is the big story, and I can't seem to write it in a way that makes anyone else really care about it. That was very hard."

The self-reflection that makes Wickersham's writing so accessible to her readers infuses her next words. "In hindsight, I think that not selling it was the best thing that could have happened. If I had sold it, it would have been a so-so novel. Very numb." Her face breaks into a knowing smile. "I was trying to make the experience be lyrical, and it was not a lyrical experience. The book I'd written was not true to the experience."

She also started to see a trend in the comments from editors. "I was starting to hear the same thing over and over. People liked the writing, they liked the material, but they felt that it just wasn't focused. And what was interesting to me is that some of the things that people pointed out that didn't work were the sections that I had invented the most."

Wickersham is candid about the fact that she was working hard to keep a safe distance from the true impact her father's suicide had on her. "I wasn't being very honest with myself," she admits. And so, feeling that the project was a painful failure, she put the writing away for a while.

About a year and a half after she'd set aside the novel, she was awarded a fellowship to the MacDowell Colony in Peterborough, New Hampshire, so she decided to take the novel manuscript with her and try revising it there. For the first time, she opened herself up to looking at the experience authentically. "I think I'd gotten the stamp of approval to work on this," she explains. "It felt safe. It felt private. I felt supported. But at the same time, I was left alone."

I understand exactly what she means. This is not unlike what it feels like to be writing within the structure of a low-residency MFA program. The real work of writing has to be done on your own, but you have support waiting in the wings if you need it.

At MacDowell, Wickersham tore apart the draft of her novel manuscript. "I went through it section by section and I made a to-do list, and the list basically consisted of, okay, first chapter, throw out; second chapter, throw out; third chapter, keep these seven pages but throw out the rest." Of the close to four hundred pages she'd had, she only kept about seventy. "People have asked me if that was hard to do, and it wasn't. It actually was so exciting to do because I knew that it wasn't true. I knew that it wasn't emotionally true." Wickersham's face lights up with the enthusiasm of her speech. "It was amazing to start over with only those pieces that felt true and then just to keep thinking about how to write it."

The pieces she uncovered were not told in a linear fashion. And, she realized, neither was her father's suicide. When she stopped thinking about his death in a chronological way, Wickersham felt that she unlocked the story. In a section of the memoir appropriately titled "Suicide: deviation from chronological narrative of," Wickersham writes: "The story of my father's death—what I think led up to it, and the impact it had on my family—is a messy one. [. . .] If you take it year by year—chronologically—not much happens. It's when you begin to look at it thing by thing that the story starts to emerge."

"It was paralyzing for me to think in terms of a book," Wickersham is quick to explain. "One of the other things that happened at MacDowell is that I decided to just do it in pieces and not worry about how the pieces were going to fit together for then. Just let it be the pieces."

Just let it be the pieces: a good mantra for new writers of memoir frustrated by the struggle to puzzle together a structure. Start with a piece. Which is exactly what Wickersham did. "The first piece I wrote was a piece about money in my husband's family and how my father must have felt to juxtapose his own business struggles and failures with these other people having all this money. And so I just decided I was going to write about that, and that was the first piece."

Despite the painful nature of the material, this revelation of how to look at her story made Wickersham finally feel connected to the writing in a way she hadn't been before. "Even though it was incredibly painful, I was feeling this utter excitement. It was joyous. I knew that this writing was expressing what I needed to express. I had been flailing and then I was in there," she explains.

Even though she'd gained confidence in knowing she was at last facing the experience of her father's death the way she needed to, "being in there" was a raw and frightening experience for Wickersham. "You can't write a family memoir without writing about people in your family. Your experience is all tangled up with theirs." And writing about that tangle was one of the most emotionally difficult parts of the experience. "No matter how scrupulously you portray your family in a family memoir, you're distorting, because everybody has a lot invested in their way of seeing what happened." Wickersham goes on to say, "You have to think about honor, in a way. I know that there are things in my book that are probably hard for people in my family, but I don't think that there's anything in there that is gratuitously nasty. I didn't want it to be nasty, both for my family but also because I've read memoirs like that—where you feel like there's kind of an axe to grind—and it always makes me back away from the memoir and not really trust the writer."

"How much, if any, of the writing in process did you share with your family?"

"None," Wickersham responds emphatically. "Absolutely none. I didn't tell anybody [apart from her husband] I was writing the book. I didn't tell anyone else in my family until I sold it."

"That's brave," I respond.

Wickersham laughs. "Well, it's brave in one way; it's chicken in another way. It's interesting because I feel like I've talked to so many writers about this subject, and it's fascinating to me that there are all gradations of that. There are people who almost write in cooperation with their families. I couldn't have done that. There are also people who run the manuscript by the family and ask permission. The only person that I really checked in with was my son because he was nineteen when the book was sold. So I checked in with him periodically to make sure he was okay with things. But I couldn't really check with my mother and my sister because I think they would have said, 'Don't do it.'"

Wickersham confesses that the biggest struggle on the family front was dealing with the tension between wanting to tell the story authentically and not wanting to betray her father: This gentle man she'd known and loved, who listened to classical music, had a passion for sailing, and made her pancakes on the Saturday mornings of her childhood. This extremely guarded man who perfected the art of hiding important emotions; his turmoil and despair over failed business ventures and financial troubles, and his deep-rooted feelings of inadequacy and shame from a painful childhood. This unrecognizable man who woke up one morning when he was sixty-one years old, dressed for work, left a cup of hot coffee on the bedside table next to his sleeping wife, went into his study, shut the doors, and shot himself in the head.

"My father was an intensely private man," Wickersham tells me. "I think if he could come back, he would absolutely be appalled that I wrote this book."

I ask her how she'd managed to convince herself to keep going even though she understood this reality.

"I came to a point where I said, 'I'm damned if I'm going to let him dictate the terms of this,'" Wickersham replies. "He did this thing, whether it was a choice or out of illness, I don't know. I don't think you ever really know with suicide." Her voice holds a touch of defiance. "I'm not going to abide by a contract of silence. He broke his contract, so I'm going to break my contract. I felt that I had the right to tell it." She pauses, a thoughtful look crossing her features. "I've never said that before."

Family rules are never easy to break. "How did you deal with those moments of fear and risk?" I ask.

"Sometimes it just felt shitty," she confesses. "Especially the parts that dealt with the impact on me. I had so much trouble seeing what it had done to me. And it felt shitty for a long time. And it was depressing, and it was hard." There were ways she managed to cope, though. She credits her husband Jay's unwavering support as her primary source of strength. "He always felt that this was a book that needed to be written and was going to be written." She also found it helpful to face the self-doubt head-on in her writing. At the top of the page, she'd write things like "What am I trying to do here?" or "What am I so scared of?" and then she'd list her litany of fears: "I'm afraid people will think that this isn't interesting." "I'm afraid people will think my father was weak." "I'm afraid people will think I'm whiny." Wickersham thinks that these deliberate looks at her doubts often led her to deeper levels of meaning. "Also, when I'm writing, I try to just write alone and worry about the publishing part later," she explains. "My feeling is you can write whatever you want, and then you think about it again when it's time to publish."

"So at this point, were you thinking about the index structure?" I ask.

"The structure was the last thing," she says. "I wanted a structure for comfort, but I couldn't find that structure. I didn't want to impose something gimmicky, so I'm glad I waited and let the index emerge. If I'd started with the index, the book wouldn't have the organic feeling that I hope it does."

The index format of the book emerged from a chapter called "Numbness: An Index," one of two specifically about the psychological impact her father's suicide had on her. Wickersham had written it in short, alphabetized sections told in the second person. Having found this way to express that numbness without making the writing numb felt like a breakthrough. What if she took the whole book and made it an index? She wondered. There was something about that index form that fittingly captured the nature of the experience. "Suicide is messy and chaotic," Wickersham explains. "The index came out of that struggle that there is no way to put it in an order. So let's just plop this numb thing on top of it. The numbness contained the emotion, and the structure contained the chaos. It was an armature, and that was incredibly comforting."

The distinctive structure of Wickersham's memoir, and the earnestness of her search to understand what happened to her father and, ultimately, what happened to her, earned her book critical praise. *The Suicide Index* received numerous accolades and awards, most notably its selection as a finalist for the 2008 National Book Award.

"There's been a really lovely response from other writers," Wickersham tells me. "They understood the structure and the writing and really responded to that."

Wickersham says that she's encountered some difficulties in gaining widespread readership, though. "Partly because of the title, which I felt very strongly about, and partly because of the subject matter, a lot of people recoil." Some, she thinks, see the title and say, "Ew, a book about suicide, I don't want to read that."

"I don't really think it is a book about suicide," Wickersham quickly adds. "I think it's a book about memory and a book about storytelling and a book about families. But it's called *The Suicide Index*, so I think that's what people hear. I think there are people who are just afraid of it or repelled by the idea of it, which is sad because I don't think it is a grim book. It's about a grim thing, but it's not a grim book." I agree wholeheartedly. There's love and beauty and power and understanding woven through the pages of this exquisite book.

Wickersham's courage to tell this story frankly has given words to what is for so many an inarticulate experience. "I've gotten a lot of letters from people who have had suicide in their family," she tells me. "I actually find it very moving. There's something so lonely and isolating about being in a family where there's been a suicide. People feel like the way that they are experiencing grief is not the way that they are 'supposed' to feel." Many of her readers have found camaraderie and a sense of sharing. "They read this book and they recognize that I'm recognizing the weirdness of the experience in the same way they recognize the weirdness of the experience, and they haven't really had words for it. There's something really comforting in acknowledging that this is so weird. You never figure it out. You never really get over it."

I ask, "Was the response and impact of your story overall different than what you'd anticipated?"

Wickersham weighs her answer, then says, "In some ways it was a bigger response than I expected. Certainly the National Book Award nomination made a lot of people read it who would not have known about it otherwise." She stops and grows thoughtful. "If you've been a writer for years and years and years, which I had, and I'd been stuck on this book for years and years and years, and I had also felt such self-doubt while I was working on it and real doubt that it would ever be published, and real doubt that I would ever do it justice, so, to have that kind of affirmation was utterly wonderful. That was bigger than I had dared to hope for."

Wickersham is honest about some of the harder implications of sharing her story with others. "There are ways that you've lost access to it as your own experience. You are trying to make something coherent out of chaos, but then you lose the realness and the joy and the unpredictability of that chaos. And I feel like I turned my father into this guy in the book."

Returning to her earlier discussion of people's fear of the topic of suicide, Wickersham says, "I wasn't prepared for how frightened people would be of the subject matter, and in a way, that kind of made me mad. And I think the reason it made me mad is it felt to me like my father was becoming a pariah all over again. People would come up to me and say, 'What have you written?' and I'd say, 'I've written this book about my father's suicide,' and they would back away from me as if I'd thrown up on their shoes. I felt angry on my father's behalf. This is part of the complexity of humanity, and this person's sort of saying, 'Sorry, too much.'"

Stigma. Another subject that resonates with me at a very close level. I understand how it feels when people back away.

These moments of disappointment in the midst of the positive response to the memoir nurtured some healthy defiance for Wickersham. "I felt very protective of the book, of the subject, and, still, of my father in a way."

"Did the overall process of telling this story change the way you felt about it?"

"For me, it didn't haunt me in the same way. That desperate need to write about it got quenched." She tells me about a piece she once read about a police sketch artist. "She said that one of the things she liked about her job was that before meeting her, these people had to carry the memory of that face, but that once they gave it to her, she was hoping that maybe they could start to forget it a little bit." Similarly, Wickersham feels that if she hadn't written the book, she'd be in the same place she'd been. Writing the book helped move her to a different place. "I didn't have to dwell on the gory details in the same way. I wasn't responsible for remembering them any more in the same way. I can remember my father without always thinking about the way he died, without always feeling it like a punch in the gut." She felt like she'd written the book she'd wanted to write, and there was a peace that accompanied that feeling. "Books tend to grow out of obsessions, and there's a way that you work through those obsessions. It's not that it leaves you, but you are not obsessed with it in the same way. The obsession burns itself out."

I often wonder if I will ever stop feeling the urge to share my story, even after it's written. And then I wonder how I possibly ever could, because it has so definitively shaped the person I am, and I can't imagine that it won't continue to do so. But maybe by writing it, like Wickersham has hers, I can be shaped in a different way that moves me to a different place, too.

Wickersham has written beyond her hard story and entered new stories. Her latest book, *The News from Spain: Seven Variations on a Love Story*, is a collection of stories linked by the imperfect and indefinable nature of love. NPR named it a Best Book of 2012.

"This book, though," Wickersham says pointing to my copy of *The Suicide Index*, resting between us on the table, "is where I really learned to be a writer. I finally understood the difference between writing a story that was alive under me and writing a story that was fake and dead."

I sit across from her, fully engaged in our continued dialogue about her memoir. I sense in the occasional pauses in conversation and the far-away gaze in her deep brown eyes that the story of her father's suicide is still something Wickersham carries. I recognize that stories like hers and stories like mine aren't ever fully resolvable. She ends *The Suicide Index* saying as much: "I could end this book in a lot of different places, just as I began by circling, over and over, back to the day of my father's death. [. . .] Knowing that I'll never know the whole story. Knowing that I'll never feel his death as fully and directly as I might wish to; and that perhaps as a result I'll never be done feeling it."

Maybe this is how stories like Wickersham's and stories like mine and the stories of so many others need to be told: with their edges blurry and their endings unfixed, leaving us with just enough room to keep on telling them.

CHAPTER 5

Kyoko Mori

· *The Dream of Water*
· *Yarn: Remembering the Way Home*

Within two minutes of our first meeting, on a morning in September 2015, Kyoko Mori, the acclaimed author of fiction and nonfiction, is balancing her Burmese cat, Jackson (short for the singer Jackson Browne, "because he's brown," she explains), on her head and showing me how she can wear him like a hat. I immediately recognize that, despite her impressive backstory, this petite woman, dressed comfortably in jeans and a navy-and-red-striped t-shirt with a polka dot pocket, her long, dark hair hanging loosely past her shoulders, does not take herself too seriously.

Mori has just given me a quick tour of her stunning third-floor apartment in a stately red-brick building nestled amid nineteenth-century homes in Washington, DC's Cleveland Park neighborhood. Characterized by high ceilings, architectural nooks and shelves, and a fabulous floor–to-ceiling bookcase with a rolling ladder filling the entire back wall of her living room, the cozy apartment feels ideal for a writer. I don't have to stretch too hard as I scan the space to figure out that Mori is a passionate admirer of cats, birds, and flowers. Wooden boxes with colorful blossoms adorn the exterior of her tall back windows, a humming-bird feeder hanging over the top. An eclectic mix of artwork scatters her walls: watercolors, ink sketches, and tapestries, featuring the aforementioned cats and birds and flowers.

Unlike his extroverted brother, Mori's second cat, Miles, a sleek blue-point Siamese (named for blues musician Miles Davis, "because he's 'kind of blue'"), runs to hide in a closet at the first sight of me. In a while he'll warm up and dig through my bag until he finds a scrap of paper to pull out and chew. Later, both cats will charm me with their repertoire of tricks—a routine of leaping over plastic sticks, jumping through hoops, and climbing up shelves at Mori's commands. Her deep affection for and devotion to these cats is obvious. She admits midway through our conversation, "My whole adult life has been a process of understanding that I really don't like to travel. I like to stay in one place, you know?" A big reason for that, she tells me, is that she hates to leave her cats.

Paradoxically, though, the theme of displacement has been at the core of Mori's writing, particularly her nonfiction. Her two memoirs, *The Dream of Water* and *Yarn*, and her collection of essays, *Polite Lies*, all share the thread of her life spent straddling two very different cultures and trying to determine where she belongs.

Mori was born in Kobe, Japan, in 1957. When she was twenty, she moved on her own to the United States to study writing, attending Rockford College in Illinois for her undergraduate degree and receiving a master's and PhD in creative writing from the University of Wisconsin-Milwaukee. She spent much of her adult life in the Midwest, just outside of Green Bay, writing and teaching at St. Norbert College, until she received a prestigious five-year appointment as Briggs-Copeland Lecturer at Harvard University and moved to Boston. She later moved to Washington, DC, and is now a full professor in George Mason University's MFA program and also teaches in Lesley University's low-residency MFA program.

The story that propelled Mori six thousand miles from her Japanese homeland is rooted in trauma. When she was twelve years old, Mori's beloved mother put a plastic bag over her head, unhooked the gas line, held it to her mouth, and killed herself. Two months later, her father moved his mistress into their home, and for the next eight years, Mori was cut off from her mother's family and endured physical and emotional abuse from her father and stepmother. Her move to the United States was, in all senses of the word, an escape.

In 1990, during a sabbatical, Mori took her first trip back to Japan since her departure thirteen years earlier. She toured the country, including her hometown, and spent time with relatives, many of those on her mother's side whom her father had forbidden her to see so many years before—aunts, uncles, cousins, and her ninety-four-year old grandmother. "I came away from those visits thinking I was going to write a novel," she tells me. She'd just finished her first novel, *Shizuko's Daughter*, a coming-of-age story set in Japan that, in many ways, parallels her own coming-of-age story, and had contracted with an agent. "What I was going to write now was going to be almost like a prequel to *Shizuko's Daughter*, about the older people in the family."

Mori's mother's family was deeply affected by the events at the end of World War II. They lost their land, their livelihood, their entire city destroyed by firebombs. Mori was born only twelve years after the war ended, and the specter of its impact was embedded in the childhood stories she remembers from her mother and grandmother. "So I wanted to write about that, you know?" she says, tucking a foot under her other leg as she relaxes into her chair across from where I sit on the couch.

The more she talks, the more I notice the distinctions in Mori's speech. Her words still carry traces of her Japanese accent, but her inflection and dialect are distinctly Midwestern. She peppers her talk with "you know?" as a habitual punctuation to her points. "But, because I hadn't experienced it," she continues, "I couldn't even imagine, you know? It would be easier to write a historical novel about, like, five centuries ago than a historical novel about an event you kind of missed just by a few years. So I couldn't do it. And then I was going to write nonfiction about it, but for the same reason, I couldn't. I realized: who am I to write their story?"

Mori had to reevaluate her purpose: if not these stories she'd had in mind, then what? "I kind of wasted my sabbatical writing things that were never quite right, but I think I had to write all of that to get to the right place."

It took her some time to recognize that the "right place," the real story, the big story—the story about going back to Japan and realizing that in no way could it ever be her home—had been there from the moment she boarded the airplane. "I really think that so much of writing a book, especially the first part, is like avoidance," she explains. "You avoid the real story because at once you think it's too painful and too boring. I mean, some days, I think, God, I don't want to go there because it's too painful. But most of the time, I think, God, it's too boring." She tilts her head back and laughs. "That is like a deadly combination when you think of the most painful thing that happened in your life as being kind of boring, you know? Who wants to hear that?"

The question of whether people would be interested in reading this story was coupled with the question of how Mori was going to write it. Though she'd written a few essays by this time, she didn't feel completely at ease in the nonfiction genre. "I hadn't written a lot of nonfiction and definitely not a book-length narrative."

"So how did you get started on it?"

"I was always a fiction writer who heavily based stuff on things that I experienced, and I was always in the habit of writing in my journal. So, when I was in Japan, I had a journal that I wrote in, like a notebook, and then I also had kind of like an appointment calendar, where I wrote down where I went and just a few comments. So, between those two, I had a really good record of what I did every day."

Operating from a fiction mindset, though, Mori needed to figure out the plot that would drive the story from beginning to end. "I always think plot has to rise out of character, and that is exactly the same whether it's fiction or nonfiction. It's really about that person realizing something or working toward something or coming to terms with something. There has to be conflict, you know?"

Mori's journey to Japan was rife with conflict: encounters with friends and relatives she hadn't seen for years, revelations about both her mother and her father, palpable reminders of her life before and after her mother died, a painful reunion with her father and stepmother. She still struggled, though, to find a way to tell it that would be authentic. She was still avoiding. It was only when she decided that she really had to tell two stories to write this memoir—the story about her journey to Japan in 1990 and the story of her past—that the writing opened up for her. "I finally kind of saw the whole structure. Now I was writing with a purpose. I was going in the right direction. Whatever I was writing, even though there would be a lot that would change, I wasn't just taking a stab in the dark."

"So what was it like for you as you began writing about this journey and revisiting the painful history that it unearthed?"

"By then, I was so relieved to not have to be writing a novel I couldn't finish or writing about people that I couldn't keep interviewing because they lived in Japan. I was so relieved that I had everything I needed for this because it was in my journal, it was in my memory, and I also had artifacts—letters written by different members of my family in the past. I had those in a box along with photographs. I was just so relieved that I didn't have to go anywhere else to collect any more material."

For Mori, the writing became a kind of reprieve at a time in her life when she felt restless and self-conscious. "My whole life in Green Bay, I realize in retrospect, was [that] I never really felt like myself. I was such a minority in every way: as an educated woman, a Japanese American, a writer in my department at the college where I was the only writer. I just felt like I was on TV somehow as a kind of strange, peculiar phenomenon."

She had a writing studio in her basement. "When I went down there to write," she explains, "and it was just me and the writing and Dorian (her cat who lived for close to eighteen years) who just came and sat next to me, I felt great. Finally I got to be myself. So, I don't think I cared so much about the fact that the material was hard. Just living was hard."

That Mori had experience and saw herself as a writer also helped her through the process. "I did worry that nobody might read it, but I didn't really worry that I shouldn't be writing it, because if it didn't work out, nobody was going to read it, so how would it hurt anyone?"

I reflect on the fact that most of the people involved in Mori's first memoir live in Japan and speak Japanese, and there was a high probability that they would not read the story Mori was writing. "Was there a certain level of safety because of that?" I ask her.

"Completely," she replies. "They wouldn't read it, and I knew I could elect not to have it be translated into Japanese." She adds, "It never was." She leans over to pick Jackson up from where he's insistently brushing back and forth against her leg. She smushes his face against hers and then settles him on her lap. "The thing is," she says, running her hand absently across Jackson's back, "these were all the people who had all the power when I was a child. And I had no power as a child. So no matter what I said about them as an adult, it couldn't even begin to tip the balance. I felt like they kind of owed me, you know? I didn't talk twenty years ago. It was now my turn to talk."

I think of so many of the other writers I've spoken with who've talked about this same determination to find their voices, despite the rules that might silence them. "Do you think we all have to launch some sort of rebellion against the family rules when we write these stories?" I wonder aloud.

"When you write about somebody, you are taking control. When you, as the writer, sign on for this, you kind of just have to accept this is how it's going to be." Mori laughs. "I just think that anyone who marries or goes out with a writer, they should understand that they are signing up for this. I would love to say to people when I associate with them, 'Don't worry, I'll never write anything about you,' but it would just not be true. So you might as well forget that."

Mori gestures toward my copy of *Yarn*, her most recent memoir, lying on the coffee table. This narrative is a literal weaving together of her own history with the history of the creative art of knitting, set against the backdrop of the quiet dissolution of her marriage and her eventual departure from Wisconsin. "Writing about my parents was totally different than writing about my ex-husband. Entering into that [the story of their marriage] was so hard. How can I write about somebody I spent so much time with? And the upshot is that we're not together, and how can I do it in a way that's respectful? I was so much more careful in *Yarn* not to say anything that I hadn't already said to Chuck, not to portray him in a way that would be surprising to him or anyone else. I would never reveal anything about him that everybody didn't already know. We had a good relationship. We still do, even though we haven't seen each other in a long time. We've always been in touch in some way." She pauses, her face serious, obviously thinking through her next words. "I think this is the idea that this is a person I chose to associate with, and I can't walk away thinking that I didn't respect him enough to treat him with dignity."

Mori reiterates that the same contract is not true with everyone in her life. "With my parents, I didn't ask to be their child. So writing about them was totally different. My mother made her choice to die, and she died. It wasn't necessarily Chuck's choice for me to leave."

In both *The Dream of Water* and *Yarn*, Mori lays bare some heartrending moments from her childhood: Coming home to find her mother dead and then being left alone with her mother's body while her father goes to meet the doctor. Suffering silently through her own grief, while her father upends her whole world with the introduction into their home of his hateful and manipulative mistress. Meticulously following a nightly routine of propping chairs up between the door of her bedroom and her bed and scattering books and tennis balls on the floor to act as deterrents for her father and give her time for escape if he made good on his ongoing threats to stab her with a meat knife. Mori also guides us through the painful realities of coming to terms with many of these experiences and trying to understand their influence on the person she is today. I ask her how difficult it was for her to give words to these experiences.

"I think they were not quite as difficult only because I thought about them all the time anyway. I think when a reader reads something like that, they're reading it for the first time. But when you are writing it, you've already thought about it so many times. Which is why sometimes it seems like it's even almost boring. It's not shocking to you because you already know it so well."

Mori is pragmatic about the emotions the writing did stir up. "In writing about it, I realized that I was still sort of mad about it in ways I never thought I was." She chuckles. "But I also never expected to feel better about any of this stuff after writing it because if that were the case, writers would be like the best adjusted people in the world."

For Mori, the "feeling better" part happened with the satisfaction of completing the book itself. "I didn't feel better about what happened, but I felt better about the book. It was like a substitute."

Finding the right shape and structure for both of her memoirs was a lengthy and solitary struggle. Mori's not someone who shares her writing in process. And, she admits, she's not someone who confides in people when something in her life is in process. "I think it is a personality thing," she explains. "And a Midwestern thing," she adds. "When I make major decisions, I don't usually talk about it until I'm pretty sure I'm going through with it. Then I might tell a couple of people. I like to figure it out on my own.

I'll let you know when I figure it out." The page becomes Mori's confidante. "The impetus for writing really is so that then you can talk about your feelings."

When the manuscript is finished and sent, Mori explains, "then it's done. Now I can talk about what it was, and to finish it and find a publisher. That was a huge big thing. I felt great. I was finally done. Now I could go do something else."

Even though she's gone on to do those "something elses," her other stories, in various ways, still contain morsels of her backstory. I ask her about that ongoing confluence. "There are just sort of certain touchstones in your life that you always have to come back to—you know, the place from which all of your writing originates. My mother's death was definitely one of those for me. The decision for her to die. And, also, the decision for me, in some ways, to let it happen. I mean, I knew she was going to do it. I knew I couldn't stop her. And I wanted her to know that I was going to be okay without her. That is such a touchstone for me, that moment of letting her go."

Jackson jumps off Mori's lap to investigate what Miles is doing with the paper he's nabbed from my bag. "I think this is where nonfiction is like fiction, in that there are things you realize later and you layer it back in. You know, the stuff you did not articulate to yourself then." She explains that in these realizations, the world becomes a bigger place with broader possibilities.

"Did this broadening of thinking change your feelings about your story when it was finally in print?"

With the same pragmatism as earlier, Mori answers, "I think I became more solidified in everything I said because it was out there. It wasn't like I saw things more clearly, but everything I said, I couldn't take back. Here was the official version. An official version for me, too."

I tell Mori my personal fears that putting my story in print will box me into being that person on the page. "Do you ever worry that people will assume these 'official versions' are the only versions of who you are?"

"I don't really worry about it. Even if it's a recent book, I think anybody who reads should understand that the most fundamental thing about writing is that the persona in the book is not all of who you are. Even right now. It's like a part of who you are, strengthened many times."

She tells me about how her first novel, *Shizuko's Daughter*, a *New York Times* notable book, was first translated into German and then Korean, even before it was translated into Japanese. "That, for me, is a metaphor of what it's like to be read. Even when somebody's reading the book in the language you actually wrote in, it is like translation in that you cannot be standing looking over their shoulder making sure they understand everything you really meant and nothing else. You have to sort of give up this idea that you can control everything."

Mori cautions that assessing reader response can be an overwhelming prospect. "I think I came to totally lower my expectations about how people are going to read my work once I put it out there." She's also selective about her own responses to what readers say about her writing. "I do read the reviews, whether they are good or bad. And I totally care what my friends think. But all my close friends are writers, so what they think about the books is different from what somebody thinks about the books who is not a writer."

She immediately qualifies, "I'm always honored that people would share their personal stories with me about how they too had to overcome their parent's death or suicide, but then I feel like I also need to step back from that. I'm glad that people read the books and feel that they are helpful, and I certainly wouldn't write anything that would be hurtful."

Jackson has joined Miles in a new search through my bag for more paper. Mori leans over to playfully shoo them away. When she turns back to me, she says, "I guess 'do no harm' is really kind of my philosophy about writing. I hope, in some general way, everything I do contributes to the positive energy in the universe, but the reason for my writing is that I like doing it. I like to sit down at my desk and kind of arrange things. And some days, I don't even enjoy that. But I feel compelled to sit at the desk and rearrange things until I like the way the pattern looks. That is important to me. I hope that I'll write things that people would find helpful, but in a way, I'm happier when people find the design to be beautiful than the content to be helpful." She pauses. "I would feel really terrible if somebody thought I did not write well. That would break my heart. I want something beautiful in the end that I can look at and say, 'I made that.'"

Despite the much-deserved success she's achieved in her writing career, with seven books and numerous essays to her name, and the countless times she's sat down at her desk to begin the process of writing something new, Mori still admits the "making" is truly the hardest part. "I continue to be surprised every time I sit down to do it how much you have to write and revise to get a book. And each time, this is the thing I have to forget. Any time I start a new book, I can't be thinking too much about how much of what I'm writing is or is not going to be in the book by the time I'm done. Forgetfulness is great."

I point again to my copies of *The Dream of Water* and *Yarn* and ask, "Do you ever look at these stories and ask, 'Did I get it right?'" I'm speaking to my own insecurities now by asking this question, my fears that no matter how hard I try to recount my experience with my dad's illness and death, I won't ever be able to do the whole story the justice I feel it deserves.

"By the time that was the question, I think I realized that the part I had to get right really wasn't about anyone else; it was really about me," Mori replies. "I would never really know what my mother's story was, or my relatives' reaction to it, or my father's even. The thing I had to get right was me trying to figure that all out. Once I realized that, then really what mattered was that I do my best."

Mori seems to understand that this final question I'm asking is more about me than it is about her because she shifts to a gentle tone I imagine her using with her own writing students who are struggling to bring their experiences to the page. "These things already happened," she says. "Whatever you do with it is yours. And if these bad things that happened in your family enable you to write a book that is going to be the ticket to the next part of your life, I don't think that there is any guilt or shame in this, because those things already happened. While they were going on, you reacted in the way you reacted with the best of intentions, probably not always doing the right thing. And when you write the book, it will be the continuation of that. You'll have the best of intentions, and not always do the right thing in terms of craft or in terms of the storytelling or even in terms of getting it published. But you are going to do your best, and what more can you do?"

Later that night, I replay this section of the interview when, on my flight home from DC, I relax into my window seat and pop in my ear buds to check the quality of the recording. I have plans to listen to the whole thing in the coming days, so I only rewind the last few minutes. I watch the expanse of lights from our nation's capital disappear into the night below the clouds and allow Mori's voice to quiet my mind. "Do your best. What more can you do?" I lean my head back against the headrest and close my eyes. There is nothing else for me to see beyond the dark out the window.

CHAPTER 6

Richard Hoffman

· *Half the House*
· *Love & Fury*

Inside Changsho Restaurant in Cambridge, Massachusetts, the lunchtime din of voices and the clamor of utensils and dishes reverberate through the space. I'm wishing now that I'd spoken up and asked for a more secluded seat when the host guided poet and author Richard Hoffman and me to this table less than ten feet from the bustling, all-you-can-eat buffet filled with steaming bins of wonton soup, crab Rangoon, spring rolls, dumplings, fried rice, General Gau's chicken, and bowls of fresh fruit and varied desserts.

Hoffman seems unfazed by the decibel level, made even louder by a boisterous table of business-attired professionals next to us. He orders a bowl of hot and sour soup, and I decide to let my anxiety about the distractions go. Within minutes of beginning our conversation about his memoir, *Half the House*, I am so immersed in his story that the surrounding ruckus fades into a distant hum of white noise.

This distinguished man sitting across from me wearing a tweed jacket and raising a spoonful of steaming liquid toward his whiskered face—senior writer in residence at Emerson College, author of three collections of poetry, a collection of short stories, numerous essays, and about to launch his new memoir, *Love & Fury*, when we meet in June 2014—is no stranger to the struggle of telling a hard story. His first memoir, *Half the House*, is a courageous and beautifully written account of the darkness and light of his blue-collar upbringing in 1950s Allentown, Pennsylvania. He grew up in a family of four boys, two of whom were terminally ill with muscular dystrophy. Hoffman's is a story of grief, of silence, of shame, of endurance, of resilience, of understanding, of redemption. And, after its publication, it became an extraordinary story of justice.

As many memoirists do for the sake of clarity, Hoffman begins his book with a simple statement about the veracity of the facts and events he portrays. He then writes, "I have, in most instances, altered the names of persons outside my family. In one instance, on principle, I have not."

The man Hoffman names directly is Tom Feifel, Hoffman's former football and baseball coach, a man who inflicted brutal sexual abuse on Hoffman, including raping him, when he was ten years old. For Hoffman, writing about this trauma was necessary to portraying his authentic life on the page. It was an important part of his story and a secret he'd carried into adulthood. In an afterward included in a republished edition of the memoir, Hoffman writes, "It was the decision, on principle, not to change the name Tom Feifel that proved to be fateful. There was simply no reason to protect him. I did not foresee anything like what happened. I had no incendiary intentions. I pictured him, if indeed he was still alive, as old and pathetic, living alone, surrounded by stacks of porn magazines."

Indeed, Feifel was still alive. He was still coaching. And he was still abusing young boys. In Allentown, no less, where he'd brutalized Hoffman more than thirty-five years earlier. Soon after its publication, a copy of *Half the House* landed in the hands of a mother whose son was playing on a team coached by Tom Feifel and who, she discovered, was Feifel's latest victim. Thus began a chain reaction that led to Feifel's arrest and imprisonment. He died in prison seven days after *Dateline NBC* aired a segment featuring Hoffman and his father speaking about the impact of *Half the House* on this criminal case. Investigators, who found what they called a "museum of pornography" in Tom Feifel's home after his arrest, believe that Feifel sexually abused more than 450 boys in his lifetime.

Richard Hoffman's courageous decision to write his memoir, and to name his abuser, made the abuse stop.

Though I can't deny being intrigued by the true-crime nature of the drama that played out because of Hoffman's memoir, it's the story of his journey to write it in the first place that keeps my attention long after the lunch rush clears out and we are the only two diners left amidst the empty tables scattered throughout the restaurant.

Hoffman describes the path to tell his story as "completely an accident" that curved into "a nineteen-year arc" beginning in 1976 and progressing until *Half the House* was published, in 1995. Hoffman was a poet by inclination and training, but he came to a point where he wasn't really able to write. "I didn't understand why because I had the usual macho 'I can just ride over everything' ambition," he tells me. Looking back now, he can laugh and say, "Well, duh, within a three-year period I had lost two of my brothers and my grandmother, who was beloved, and also a favorite teacher, a mentor of mine who I was very close to. It was like a dark star where it implodes. I was just imploded with grief."

Back then, that implosion often took the form of self-destructive behavior. Hoffman talks candidly about his alcoholism. "I was in the habit of abandoning myself," he recalls. "Here there's psychic pain or there's oblivion. Ah, I'll take the oblivion please. Let's just get hammered. Let's have a good time. And like many in the culture, I called it pleasure."

He enrolled in graduate school at Goddard College hoping the instruction there might put him back on track with his writing.

He confesses, "I really needed somebody to take me by the hand and lead me back to my life which I had abandoned."

A mentor, the poet Stephen Tapscott, turned out to be that somebody. Hoffman laughs. "He suggested that my poems were about nothing, and they amounted to nothing, and he didn't understand why. He said, 'Look, I have met you, you feel things deeply, you can be very funny, but none of that is in the poems. What's up with that? Why are you writing these denatured kinds of little verbal machines to show off your dexterity when you're not saying anything?'"

Hoping to help Hoffman break open his work, Tapscott assigned him a task that connected to Hoffman's Catholic upbringing: write about the fourteen Stations of the Cross. "I thought, This is stupid," Hoffman admits. "But he said, 'If you want to work with me, you have to do this.'" So, Hoffman agreed, hoping to get it over with quickly and get back to what he thought he was really supposed to be doing.

Over a period of two weeks, he had to write about each station three times without looking back at what he'd written. As a result of this seemingly tedious exercise, two things happened. The first was that Hoffman began to see pages piling up beside his typewriter in a way that never happened when he was writing poetry. "The second thing that happened," he says, "is that those iconic images, which are in every Catholic church in the world, began to suggest things to me about my own life."

Somewhere around the second or third time writing about Jesus being taken down from the cross, Hoffman was reminded of his father propping his brother up in the bed when he was dying. "And the next thing you know, I'm writing about that," he says, "and all of these other things that I had never thought to write about that I had decided weren't real writing."

"You hadn't written about your brothers' deaths before?" I ask.

"Never, never. I'd written a poem or two, but they weren't exploring the thing. They were sort of markers or monuments. Elegies."

The idea of the Stations of the Cross exercise, Hoffman thought, was to open up things so that he could write poems about them. "Turns out, the prose itself became the thing." Despite the breakthrough, Hoffman felt extremely vulnerable embracing this unfamiliar writing territory and exposing portions of his family story—his story. He describes a graduate class where he first read some of these pieces. "People started weeping, and I started shaking, and the feel of the room was so different from 'Let me read you my poem and you'll be impressed.' I didn't know what to do with it—to the point where at the end of it, when people applauded, I bolted." He says it felt like he'd just stripped naked in front of the crowd. "I felt like, 'What have I done? Oh, my God! Can I put the genie back in the bottle?' I was terrified."

The valve had been released on something that felt frighteningly out of Hoffman's control, and he didn't know where to put it. "This was 1977, and there was no memoir then, no such animal. There was St. Augustine; there was Jean Jacques-Rousseau. But people weren't writing memoirs, and so I didn't know what I had done."

It wasn't until seven or eight years later, that Hoffman actually recognized he was writing a book. "I must have had some idea that I was trying to make something coherent out of it," he muses. "But I thought it would be a big essay. And then it got to be a bigger essay."

Hoffman says the same experience of not knowing he was writing a book was true for his second memoir, *Love & Fury*, in which he excavates the artifacts of his past, particularly his complicated relationship with his father, to try to understand who he is in the present. "After my father died, I realized that I had unwittingly and unintentionally declared a moratorium on writing about him anymore after *Half the House*. I felt like I'd put him through a lot with that book, and even though I didn't intentionally consider him off limits, I just didn't write about him anymore. I thought that was over. Done with. Then, when he died, a whole lot of stuff started percolating to the surface, and I realized I had to write about him again."

When the percolating continued, Hoffman went on a two-week writing retreat thinking he would come back with the draft of an essay about his father. "I had all my notes lying around on the floor of this house where I was staying alone, and I had other things tacked on the wall. I had things on the counter in the kitchen. I kept trying to make it cohere, but there would be so many different branches of it that wouldn't." He remembers the moment, when sitting on the rug with all the stuff around him, he realized what he was writing was more than an essay. "I sort of rocked back on my heels and said, 'Oh, fuck. It's a memoir.'" The trials of the memoir-writing process with *Half the House* were not something he was sure he could endure again. "I thought, I don't have nineteen more years!" Fortunately, writing *Love & Fury* only took him five. "This time, I knew what it was and what I was trying to give birth to."

On his first memoir foray, though, Hoffman felt lost. He had no map for where the writing was leading him. And, for a long time, he fought to keep all the things he was trying to express neatly contained. "I was writing two books," he explains. His memoir was the sad story of a working class family with two terminally ill kids. But he was also writing a novel in which a kid gets abused by his coach. "As I imagined the plot of that novel, it turned out that the protagonist, who is now grown, is going back to confront the abuser." He waves his fork toward one side of our table. "See, I was going to keep that over there in the fiction department." Even when a writer friend, Bill Patrick, read a draft of the novel and told him that it was part of the story taking shape in the memoir, Hoffman resisted. "Psychically, I was not ready to bring the two together. I was not ready to let my peas touch my mashed potatoes."

"So how did you know when you were ready?" I ask.

"The unlocking of it is something that happens to you," he replies. "I don't think you decide to tell it or not to tell it." He's thoughtful for a minute and then says, "I tried very hard not to write about it. Maybe putting the abuse in a novel and keeping the memoir separate was a way for me to get it written. I hadn't thought about that until just now," he reflects.

It took years of trial and error to collapse the two stories together in a way that felt truthful. "Because the process had gone on so long, I got to the point where I thought, the only honest way to tell this story is to incorporate my resistance as part of the story." So, he tried writing it from three different views: how he looked at things at twenty-five, how he looked at things at thirty-five, how he looked at things at forty." He says the editors at Harcourt Brace wanted the book, but found that structure too cumbersome. They wanted him to tell it in a more straightforward way.

"I had to find that shape," Hoffman explains. But he admits that after the initial meeting with the editors, whom he recognizes now as being absolutely right in their criticism, it took him six months to stop being angry before he could bring himself back to the project. "But after six months, I thought, Okay, let me go back at this. I started cutting it up and laying it on the floor, and once I had that opening [the book's first chapter], then it all started to fall into place."

Despite the freedom he felt in finding the right structure, Hoffman still had other battles to fight. "The arc of the classic coming–of–age story is a story of coming to terms with the past, and it ends at the point where you know that the narrator has somehow surmounted this obstacle and is going to make it. And so many people kept trying to advise me to stick to that."

That advice included leaving out one of the most poignant moments in the memoir—a pivotal chapter where Hoffman, now a father himself, confronts his father. In the chapter, Hoffman expresses his anger about the physical beatings his father inflicted on him when he was a child. That abuse created a barrier that made it impossible for him to tell his parents about Feifel's abuse, even though he suspected his father might have known about it. Hoffman also reveals to his father the long-term damage of alcoholism and drug abuse that nearly killed him. "So many people kept trying to advise me to stick to the classic narrative arc. They advised me not to put that abuse stuff in there saying, 'Oh the sad stuff is so beautiful, but nobody wants to read about that.'"

Hoffman took a defiant stand and vowed to keep all of that material despite trusted readers telling him it didn't fit, but he also recognized that if people were not getting its connection, then he hadn't sufficiently made it part of the story. So he kept rewriting until both he and those trusted readers were satisfied with how those pieces fell into place. "I feel now that it is as integral to the book as it is to the life."

"Did you intentionally leave things out of the book?" I ask.

"Oh, sure. You can't put your whole life in the book. You have to find the story and then decide what serves that story—which is why people can write second and third and fourth memoirs." This reality was clear to Hoffman when *Half the House* was published and he found there was still plenty of life material left for him to write about. Some of that has emerged as his new memoir, *Love & Fury*.

Though the trail to his first memoir was rutted and long, Hoffman didn't find the writing process to be all heartache, defiance, and despair. He had the gift of support from his wife, Kathleen Aguero, also an acclaimed poet. "To be wrestling with childhood trauma with the person that you are in love with and making a life with now is already a kind of healing, even if you are not a writer. But the fact that we're both writers was really important."

And Hoffman says that as the project gained momentum, the poet in him came back to life. "I do write for the ear," he says. Enthusiasm animates his face. "And I absolutely love that part of the process. So as difficult as some of these memories were to wrestle into clarity, there's a pleasure in doing that. There's a pleasure in making sentences. It's not telling the story. It's as if you are painting it a brush stroke at a time."

"Did recognizing that artistic side, releasing the poet in you, help you to work to the end?" I ask.

"Yes," Hoffman replies. "There's a poem by Bruce Weigl called 'The Impossible,' and he's very explicit about what happened to him—he was forced to give a man a blow job in a railroad yard when he was ten. He talks about it throughout the poem in very explicit terms and very clear terms. Then, the poem makes a turn and the last line is: 'Say it clearly and you make it beautiful, no matter what.' And I look at the title of the poem—'The Impossible.' You can never entirely redeem the experience. You can't make it not hurt anymore. But you can make it beautiful enough so that there's something to balance it in the other scale. And if you understand that word *beautiful* as not necessarily *pretty*, then you're getting close to recognizing the integrative power of restoring the balance, which is restoring the truth."

"What did it feel like to finish?"

"I felt elation," Hoffman says. "To borrow a phrase from the Dylan song, I felt like I made it into heaven before they shut the door." Without any notes of arrogance spilling into his words, Hoffman says of the finished book, "I understood that what I had made was a work of art. I had spent all of these years fashioning this into what I hoped was going to appeal to more than people's interest in what happened, but that would move people in ways that poems move people, that the best fiction moves people. I felt pride about that. I was able to say to myself that I had done something that I thought was extraordinary. I had taken the thing that was the deepest, darkest, foulest thing that was a part of me and turned it into art."

Then he adds with a chuckle, "But then I was worried immediately that people were going to read it!"

This quandary strikes a familiar chord. I'll finish a scene and a ripple of satisfaction will flow through me because the words have fallen into place and it just feels right. Then, almost simultaneously, I'm flooded with anxiety at the thought of showing it to anyone. I share these concerns with Hoffman. He tells me he often hears the same thing in the writing workshops he teaches.

"I remind my students this same thing: writing and publishing are two different things. Don't confuse them," he cautions. "As soon as you start thinking, Well, I could never publish that, then the censor is right in the room with you with a pencil crossing stuff out as fast as you can write it. You can't work that way."

He's not the first of these writers to give me some variation of this warning. "You've come this far, so you don't have a choice," Hoffman says. "So don't think about 'Oh, can I do this? Should I do this?' You don't have a choice anymore. That train left the station a long time ago. Any thoughts that are turning around that question, just get them out of here."

Hoffman could never have expected the far-reaching effects of his memoir. I ask him what it was like to know that the person who had hurt him, traumatized him, was convicted as a direct result of *Half the House*, that his words were the catalyst.

"It felt like a deep resolution," he replies, and then hesitates, searching for the best way to articulate those emotions. "The right definition of justice. Not vengeance, not punishment, but rebalancing. He ran from the truth; the truth is here." Hoffman's voice trembles a little. "It was extremely gratifying because when I went to the trial, there were two boys who were prepared to testify against him—his two most recent victims—one was exactly my son's age at the time, and the younger boy was exactly my daughter's age. So, on a really deep level, in my *gut*, I got it. It wasn't about healing some long-ago wound of mine or any of those metaphors. It was about the fact that these kids were telling the truth *now*. They might not have to spend the next thirty years in the darkness denying what happened to them."

Hoffman does admit to being surprised and, at first, disappointed that the seventeen pages that have anything to do with abuse—"I counted," he tells me—turned out to be the way the public defined and continue to define his story. "I felt like, wait,

wait, I'm a poet; this is a literary book. But then I began to see what
a little fishbowl I was living in, in the creative writing world." He
recognized how creative writers, himself included, can become insular and mistakenly believe that the only reason other people read
our work is for the craft. "Writers need to think about connecting
to the community, to write about things that are important in their
lives that are important to the health of the community and to do it
in a way that will be taken up by the community. That's why other
people read," he says. "They read to connect."

Hoffman's connection with readers has been remarkable. And
he's come to deeply value his role as unintended spokesperson for
so many others who've endured similar experiences of abuse. In
the nineteen years since *Half the House* was first published, Hoffman has received countless letters and calls and e-mails from men
all over the world. "That continues," he tells me. "It's a trickle,
but it's a steady trickle now, all these years later. I still get three
or four letters a month." He's part of an international network
working with men all across the globe—Uganda, Cambodia, New
Zealand, England, Australia—who were abused as kids.

"Tomorrow, I'm speaking at Harvard Medical School's conference on child psychotherapy and trauma," he reveals. "What
I want to say to clinicians is don't try to sew up the wound and
send the kid back into the status quo. The child already knows,
as I did, but had no way to articulate it or express it because I had
no help, already knows a whole lot about the world than he did
the day before the trauma happened. And you need to help that
child or that person whenever they come to you to unwrite the
story that's been inscribed on them by the abuse and become the
protagonist of their own narrative once again."

At times, Hoffman has felt that having his story out in the
world makes it harder to negotiate intimacy with strangers. "People see that as a slice of your life. They don't see it as a work of
art, as a piece of something you've made. But at the same time,
what I think is most wonderful about that sort of response is that
instead of encouraging people's inner voyeur, what you get is

people who come up to you after a reading and want to tell you their story—whether it has abuse in it or not." He tells me that it's not uncommon for him to do a half-hour reading and then still be there three hours later listening to the stories of the people who've come to hear him. "You've given them permission; you've opened a door," he explains.

Hoffman doesn't deny that ongoing turmoil simmers for him just below the surface. Despite his extensive teaching and speaking experience, when he tells me about the impending talk at Harvard, he confesses, "I'm scared to death. Once we get back into that area, all of that stuff has been seared into my psyche, all of the fear and shame that comes along with trauma. It's still there. When you call that up, you go through it again. And it can be paralyzing. I think I'm better at managing it so that I can say the things that I believe must be said. And that's where the motivation comes from. It isn't about 'I need to tell my story.' It's about 'I know what must be said. And that's not about me. It's about what I'm able to see because of what I have been through.'"

Hoffman and I finally vacate the restaurant, suddenly conscious that the waitstaff is hovering close by, wanting to clear our table and prepare for the dinner rush. We leave and stand for a while on the sidewalk in front of the restaurant continuing to chat. Afternoon traffic moves along Massachusetts Avenue. Like so many of the conversations I've had on this journey, I don't want this one to end.

Hoffman begins a story about how the previous September—a few months short of his sixty-fifth birthday—he and his son went skydiving. I know the spot he references—Pepperell, Massachusetts, not far from my home in Nashua. From the soccer field where my kids play in the fall, I can see the skydiving school's colorful parachutes dotting the sky. I'm not certain how this anecdote connects to the rest of the conversation we've been having, but I'm intrigued nonetheless.

He describes the moment of standing on the ledge of the plane's open doorway waiting to jump as the instructor started the

countdown: "One. Two." Hoffman laughs and pantomimes fall-
ing off the ledge as he says, "Three." The instructor had pushed
him out the door. "He knew that if he waited for the full count and
didn't give that nudge," he explains, "I wouldn't have jumped."

Then Hoffman puts both hands squarely on my shoulders
and meets my eyes. "Three." He says and gives me a gentle push.
"Consider this your nudge forward, Melanie."

CHAPTER 7

Suzanne Strempek Shea

· *Songs from a Lead-Lined Room:*
Notes—High and Low—from My Journey
Through Breast Cancer and Radiation

The first time I met author Suzanne Strempek Shea, I was standing to the side of a dimly lit reception room in the Harraseeket Inn in Freeport, Maine, on the opening night of my first residency in the University of Southern Maine's Stonecoast MFA program. I clutched a glass of white wine like a security blanket. After spending the day sitting through orientation workshops that did more to disorient me about what to expect over the next ten days and the upcoming semester, I felt like the clichéd fish out of water. This reception was an opportunity for new students to meet faculty, but I was exhausted and anxious. All I wanted to do was go up to my room and call home to tell my husband that I'd made a horrendous mistake. That this writer scene was not for me.

And then, like a singular ray of sunshine, this tall, slim woman, her long, graying hair pulled back in a barrette, came over, put her hand on my arm, and said, "Welcome, welcome!" Just like that, I steadied.

I can't think of a better way to describe Suzanne Strempek Shea than as a walking hug. In the year and a half since that initial meeting, I've gotten to know her as teacher, mentor, and dear friend. The richness she has added to my world and the wisdom and encouragement she has brought to my work as I've waded through the often-murky waters of completing my MFA degree are immeasurable.

On this April day in 2014 that is beginning to show promises of spring, I'm visiting her in her dormered Cape Cod-style home, set back from the road on a tree-dotted hill in Bondsville, Massachusetts. She lives here with her husband, Tommy Shea, an award-winning writer himself, whom I'd had the delight of meeting a few minutes earlier when I'd arrived, and their dogs: Bisquick and Tiny. I sip from a warm mug of tea and lean against a cushion on Strempek Shea's futon in a room filled with books and windows and light. Beneath the arched entryway is a long desk with a chair at each end, two open laptops, and piles of books and newspapers—the writing space the two authors share.

Strempek Shea settles in beside me, her demeanor completely relaxed despite the "big doin's," as my father liked to say, happening in her world. A year shy of the twentieth anniversary of the publication of her first book, *Selling the Lite of Heaven*—a novel that captures many threads of her Polish-Catholic heritage—she's launching her tenth and eleventh books within six months of each other. Her sixth novel, *Make a Wish but Not for Money*, is due out in October 2014, and the month of my visit, she released *This Is Paradise*, a compelling true story about an Irish woman named Mags Riordan and the medical clinic she founded in Malawi, Africa, in memory of her son, Billy.

The account of how Strempek Shea happened upon Mags Riordan's story captures her open and engaging spirit and her wonderful gift for finding stories in almost everything. Close to thirteen years ago she and Riordan occupied adjacent craft booths at the annual Eastern States Exposition—the "Big E"—in western Massachusetts, one of the nation's largest fairs. Throughout the day, she listened to Riordan repeat the story to people who passed by her booth that her son had drowned in Africa and that she was selling her crafts to benefit the clinic she'd set up in his honor in the village where he died. Unlike most of the fairgoers who stepped away from this sad account, Strempek Shea stepped closer. She'd started her writing career working as a journalist, and her reporter's instincts told her to lean in because there was more to this woman's story. The "more" she uncovered eventually became *This Is Paradise.*

Later today, when Strempek Shea and I go over to Bay Path University, the charming baccalaureate college in nearby Longmeadow, Massachusetts, where she is writer-in-residence, I'll see *This Is Paradise* on display at the front of the bookstore.

My reason for traveling to Strempek Shea's home on this particular day, though, is to talk about another of her books: her first memoir, *Songs from a Lead-Lined Room: Notes—High and Low—from My Journey Through Breast Cancer and Radiation.* I pull out my copy and show her how I've folded the bottom corners of the pages where passages resonate in some way with me. It would be easier to count the corners that aren't folded than the ones that are.

Written with raw and self-revealing honesty, her book is a chronicle of her month and a half of daily radiation treatments after being diagnosed with breast cancer at forty-one and undergoing a lumpectomy. She shows us her isolation, her fear, her confusion, her questions, her despair. She also gives us an authentic, and often humorous, portrait of herself as patient and her distress at not measuring up to how she would have imagined. She writes, "My general upbeat, faith-filled manner would have had me guessing that if I ever got whacked by life, I'd not only look good in my hospital bed, I'd genuinely feel good, too. [. . .] 'That's just how I am,' I'd tell those who asked how I did it." When the whack actually comes, though, Strempek Shea instead cuts herself off from everyone except Tommy and a few close friends who "get it," and places a mat that says "GO

AWAY" outside her door. Her candor creates a powerful narrative of coping and recovering from a life-threatening illness, and the reality of changed perception about life that is inevitable in its wake.

"What made you decide to write about this experience as it was happening?"

She didn't start right away after her diagnosis. She had her surgery to think about, and the churning emotions that felt too hard to name. And, as she writes in her book, "Maybe it was the thing about seeing the words on the screen in front of me, which would make my problem realer than it already was."

After the first day of her radiation treatments, the impulse to write pulled Strempek Shea toward her desk. But she had no thought or intention of writing a book. "I was just thinking of myself," she says. "I came home from that first session and went upstairs to the table where Tommy and I had chairs next to each other, and Tommy said, 'How did it go?' and I went like this." She holds up her index finger. "I sat down and wrote for half an hour before I could talk."

This practice of coming home after her treatment and writing became a comforting ritual for her. "Every day when I went, I would write a little bit after the appointment, maybe for half an hour, and I got into the routine. I'd tuck things in on the weekends too. People would want to take me out somewhere or maybe I had a blah day, but there was always something I could write about." The experience dragged on with daily treatments that never let her forget she was sick. "I'm not ever comparing this to the ravages of chemotherapy—that's its constant reminder, because a lot of the time you are just feeling horrible—but here, I was taking myself to a place each and every day to do something I didn't want to do." She found release in pouring her complicated emotions about it all on the page.

Somewhere along the way Strempek Shea realized that maybe she could give what she'd written to Tommy and four or five friends who'd been supporting her since her diagnosis. "I felt like

I was very inarticulate about what I was feeling. It was really the scariest thing I'd been through, and I didn't know really what to say about it or how to say it, and in a lot of ways I wasn't myself. And then I said, 'Well, I'm best on paper.' Here I can say exactly what I was feeling and give this to them."

She thought that would be it. She'd write about the experience. She'd show her husband and friends, and then have a big bonfire with all the pages. She waited until she was finished though. By the time she showed what she'd written to Tommy, she had about 160 pages that she planned to have him and those few close friends read before she burned them. Tommy's writer's instincts told him something else. "I remember he was upstairs when he was reading it," Strempek Shea tells me, "and he turned around on the swivel chair and said, 'You know this could help other people. You should give this to your agent.'"

In a few weeks' time, I'll attend a reading for *This Is Paradise*, and I'll remember this slice of our conversation when Strempek Shea tells the audience that for each of the eleven books she's written, she can picture the exact moment when Tommy Shea told her that what she was writing about could be a book.

Despite Tommy's encouragement, the idea of showing anyone else this writing about her cancer journey was terrifying to Strempek Shea. "I thought, gosh, I don't think I could really put this out there because it's so personal." She'd written nonfiction for the fifteen years she'd worked as a journalist, but that was markedly different. She was telling other people's stories. "They weren't about anything I went through. Even though I'd written plenty of personal essays along the way, there was nothing too revealing. But these were diary entries. I felt like I didn't have any skin or any clothes. I felt like everything was exposed. I couldn't imagine putting that out for other people."

I know the feeling. That kind of exposure feels so risky when you begin writing through tough experiences. I often ask, what will people think of me when they see this? The question alone makes me want to shut my laptop and run away.

In process, the writing didn't feel so risky for Strempek Shea. "I felt like I could be very open; I could write with more abandon, because only these people who love me were going to read it." She does add that it felt uncomfortable when she was writing about things that she wasn't proud of saying or doing during her illness. "I felt like I should have been better at this somehow."

I learn that Strempek Shea and I grew up with similar mindsets about working very hard to live up to the people we are *supposed* to be. We both define ourselves as "the good girl," the one who does what's expected of her and tries not to offend anybody. So, in some ways, she admits to writing with that self-consciousness and feeling like she needed to add qualifiers that she was complaining when things could definitely have been worse. She chuckles and says one of her first thoughts about publishing this book was "I'm going to get in trouble for something."

"So what made you decide to do it?" I ask her.

The cancer diagnosis ungrounded Strempek Shea, as it would anyone, and when she learned she was going to have radiation treatment, she wanted to know what to expect. Knowing might give her some way to regain her footing. She went to the Palmer Library, near her town, but a search of the term "radiation" referred her to books on Hiroshima and Chernobyl, and "medical radiation" turned up only medical texts.

She stands, walks over to one of the many bookshelves in the room, and scans the titles. At last she picks a book and comes back to the futon with a travel book from a trip she and Tommy took. She opens to a back page where she'd handwritten notes about what they did each day. She reads, "'Day 1—Woke at 9. Walked a lot. Had cheese sandwiches.'" She laughs and taps her finger against the page, pointing to the notes, and says, "I wanted somebody's 'this.' I wanted somebody's Day 1. I wanted somebody's 'Woke at 8, stared out the window. Thought, Rats.' I thought maybe I could find some kind of guidebook, some kind of travel log [through the radiation process] that could help me. But I didn't. So I thought back to that and said, maybe I will do this." She qualifies, "It wasn't me thinking, Oh this book will be my big break and I'll make a lot of money. I was freaked out. I was confused. I thought if somebody could pick this up, even one person, and say they aren't the only one . . ." Her voice trails off, and I'm struck by the selflessness of what she's just said. She'd walk out there with no skin or clothes if it might help somebody else. This sincere kindness, expressed in everything she does, is what makes Suzanne Strempek Shea both highly empathetic and extremely relatable.

Because she was writing during her radiation therapy, Strempek Shea essentially finished the book at the same time that she finished her treatments. She says that her initial feeling was to distance herself from both. "I thought, Okay, we're done with this. Everybody's great. I've taken the trip, I've written the essay about what Cape Cod was like. We'll have a little post party, and that will be it."

But, what she discovered about her cancer experience turned out to be true for the writing about her cancer experience too. "You realize that the end of something isn't the end. It just kind of reverberates."

The reverberation of Strempek Shea's journey through illness is *Songs from a Lead-Lined Room*. And what makes this book, of the eleven books she's written, the one she admits being most proud of is the help that sharing her story has turned out to be for others going through similar experiences. "Writers look at different parts of their lives, and this was an important time in my life. I'd say I'm glad I did it for myself, but to hear things from other people, that's probably the best part. Because you want to make a difference to somebody."

That difference is giving people like me and others faced with difficult stuff permission to be who we are. Strempek Shea doesn't paint herself as a hero or a martyr. "The truth is," she says, "I didn't want this. I didn't sign up for this. None of the people you've talked to in this project signed up for this. They didn't say, 'I think I want to get sick, or I want my children to have horrible things to deal with. It's what happens, and then what do we do with it?" Writing about the experience helped her get through it, and writing about her experience has connected her to the experiences of others.

She recalls when that connection solidified for her. Not long after the book's release, she read at a small bookstore. "I remember exactly where I was in the store, and people coming up and saying either, 'I lost somebody to cancer' or, 'I know somebody' or, 'I'm going through it.' There were women with headscarves on who were going through chemotherapy. And I remember it hit me then that people are taking this [book] seriously."

She smiles and explains that the bookstore was far enough away from where she lived that the audience wasn't made up of family and friends who *had* to show up. "These were strangers, and they read about it, and they wanted to come. They not only wanted to come, but they had the book already and they left me notes. Or they stood there, and they held my hand, and they told me what they were going through. And that line was so long because people wanted to share their stories." These exchanges were not like the more generic ones she'd had with people after readings of her novels. "There was an intensity to this. I felt very honored. It's a real story and people took it as real, and they felt, here's somebody who knows something that I've been going through."

Strempek Shea recalls some responses that weren't as positive as the others, and that was when she really discovered how different it is to have someone responding to her memoir than responding to her fiction. "You hope people will get something from it, and because you got up the nerve to put it out there, you want it treated nicely. This is your baby." Her long writing career has given Strempek Shea perspective though. People are going to take from her story what they take from it. She can't dictate that. "All you can do is wish your creation well and send it out into the world."

The few discouraging interactions have been completely eclipsed by the ongoing encouragement Strempek Shea has gotten from people who tell her how valuable her memoir has been to them. Twelve years after the memoir's publication, she still keeps in touch with many of the people she met or heard from after she wrote it.

That organic power of our stories to intersect with other people's stories is what Strempek Shea has gone on to preach to her many students, me included, since writing *Songs from a Lead-Lined Room*. "The writer Anne Lamott says that when she leads workshops, she's 'evangelizing' writing. Since going through all this, I think I have become an evangelist. Books, stories, songs, art—they connect us to somebody. It boils down to you just have to do this stuff. You take what you've been through, and if you are a writer, you have to write about it."

Strempek Shea gets up and heads into the kitchen to stir the simmering pot of vegetarian soup we will soon have for lunch. Its delicious aroma wafts into the room and mingles with her resolute words that still hang in the air, words I reach for and tuck into the folds of my consciousness as a reminder of what, deep down, I already know is true. If you are a writer, you *have* to write about it.

CHAPTER 8

Abigail Thomas

· *Safekeeping: Some True Stories from a Life*
· *A Three Dog Life*

I'm fully aware that it's a crapshoot when I reach out to critically acclaimed author Abigail Thomas, and I try not to get my hopes up. From what I know about her from the background research I've done, she is a busy woman. She's the author of two memoirs, three books of fiction, three children's books, and a narrative guide about writing memoir. She's a teacher and presenter. She's a painter. She's also the mother of four, grandmother of twelve, and surrogate mother to three dogs. It's quite likely that she has very little time to focus on an MFA student's memoir-writing trials. But the good luck I've had in my efforts to connect with many of the other authors on my list and my respect bordering on worship of her memoir work prompt me to at least give Thomas a try.

I have no other means of getting in touch with her but the contact link on her website. I send my pitch, assuming the link is probably routed through her publisher or agent. I anticipate a generic courtesy response acknowledging my request and explaining the demands on her schedule. I do not expect the charming personal note, sent only two hours after my e-mail, that thanks me for my words about her books, expresses condolences for the loss of my dad, agrees to answer my questions both by e-mail and then with a follow-up phone conversation, and ends with: "You are a lovely writer, by the way. Your e-mail tells me that. Consider yourself encouraged. Yours, Abigail."

The generosity of Thomas's response shouldn't really surprise me; I've read both of her memoirs. Her kindheartedness breathes from their pages and is exactly what makes her writing so inviting to me and to so many other readers. She hands us fully examined parts of herself: her sorrows, her regrets, her joys, her insights, and she does so with unapologetic candor.

Thomas's first memoir, *Safekeeping*, published in 2000, is a fragmentary collection of brief stories that together paint a portrait of her life and her grief following the death of her ex-husband, physicist Joaquin Luttinger. The vignettes range in length from five pages to a single sentence. Each re-creates specific moments that reflect Thomas's experiences and choices, and characterize the other players in her story: her parents, her three husbands, her children, her sisters. On the surface, the scraps of memory she puts on the page seem random and sparse, but in an almost inexplicable and unexpected way, they piece together a beautifully cohesive whole: a story of motherhood, of marriage, of friendship, of mistakes, of passion, of loss, of acceptance, of wisdom. Her final line in the book, "And I know now what a moment can hold," speaks directly to this memoir's unconventional form.

A Three Dog Life, Thomas's second memoir, published in 2006, is also a nonlinear story built from shards of memory. These shards, though, materialize from one shattering event in Thomas's life—the traumatic brain injury her third husband, the late reporter and writer Rich Rogin, suffered after being struck by a car when he chased their escaped dog into the street. With wrenching honesty and sharp humor, Thomas chronicles her journey to navigate the loss of the person Rogin once was and reshape her life to accommodate the person he became—a man whose mind can no longer hold the past or look forward to the future. In the process,

Thomas somehow reshapes herself to accept and appreciate the beauty of the present.

"I don't know how non-writers of memoir survive *not* writing their memoirs," she says when she connects with me over the phone from her home in Woodstock, New York, after I explain the genesis of my project. Though she describes how she quit smoking in *A Three Dog Life*, Thomas's voice holds the husky remnants of the habit. I can't help picturing her now as she's pictured on the cover of that book: sitting on a cushiony couch, draped in a wool scarf or blanket, snuggled up against her dogs, soft light filtering into the room. "Writing the story is harder not to do," she continues. "There's no way to do it except as honestly as you can, even if it's painful."

I'm in the parking lot outside "my office," the local coffee shop where I like to work. The group of women that gathers to gossip and knit—I've christened them the "Wednesday Morning Yarn Crew"—is rowdier than usual today, so I have escaped to the quiet of my car for this conversation with Thomas.

For Thomas, writing about her experiences was never a deliberate decision. "It was a necessity," she says. "Writing is the way I try to understand. I'm hoping for clarity." She wrote *Safekeeping* in reaction to Luttinger's death, and she wrote *A Three Dog Life* as the events were unfolding in the aftermath of Rogin's accident.

"There were so many things that were happening that I didn't want to lose or forget, so writing *A Three Dog Life* kept me grounded in some way," she explains, quickly adding, "although it was impossible to stay grounded; it was impossible to stay sane."

When Thomas began writing, she thought that things were going to get better. She expected Rogin would recover. "I really didn't understand that traumatic brain injury, to the extent with which Rich had it, was going to change everything." She was, in essence, bearing witness to the events as they unfolded, so that he would understand what he'd gone through once he got better. "So, although it was very painful, there was a certain optimism in the beginning. And then that gradually changed."

When the reality of Rogin's circumstances settled in and that optimism about the outcome went away, Thomas says the writing changed. "I had to face things in myself that were very painful. The first of all being, what was wrong with me? Why couldn't I keep him home? I should be able to do this. That's when I was still kind of center stage. Why shouldn't *I* be able to do this?" It took a year or two for her to realize that nobody could do what she was asking of herself—to take care of a man in the altered condition that Rogin was in, suffering from psychosis, paranoia, hallucinations, rage. And living without the fluidity of memory.

Thomas recognized that in keeping him at home, she wouldn't be doing the best thing for her husband, and she'd be surrendering herself. "I didn't want to lose my life," she says. "I refused to sacrifice my own life to do something that I'm not equipped to do and that won't be helpful in any way at all. That was hard because I think women are bred to think, 'Oh I have to take care of whoever needs my help.' It's just that it wasn't my help Rich needed. I needed to move myself from the center and look at what Rich needed." Thomas had to understand her own limitations, face up to those limitations—despite feeling both selfish and guilty—and she had to refocus her writing to honestly reflect the complexity of those feelings.

"The single most difficult moment for me was finding myself here in Woodstock and finding myself with a life I was beginning to really like and thinking, Oh my God, if I could, would I go back to before?" And, before saying to herself that of course she'd go back, she hesitated. "There's no word to describe how I felt about myself." That moment of hesitation consumed her with guilt.

"When you hit those really tough kinds of moments of self-reflection, how did you bring yourself to put them on the page?" I ask.

"Well, there's no point if you don't, is there? There's no point," Thomas answers. "If you write a memoir, you are bound to discover things that you wish weren't true. These feelings are part of who I am. You really have to be honest and face the parts of yourself you might rather not look at. No matter how painful, it was part of my truth."

Of her guilt, Thomas says, "I had to be able to forgive myself. And I have. And that's a big deal." She laughs. "If you can forgive yourself for those difficult feelings, you can forgive anybody else almost anything."

Thomas is adamant that at the beginning she didn't consciously plan either of these memoirs to become books. "What a terrifying thought!" Nor did she intentionally plan out the fragmented structure that distinguishes both books. "The writing took the form it has now. It wasn't a plan. These books couldn't have been written any other way. This was how it was revealing itself to me. I had no choice. It was the way I experience life, in intense moments, more . . . hilarious or shameful moments that begin to add up to something, I hope."

Thomas talks of being very careful whom she shows her writing to in process. "My agent, who is also my oldest and best friend, I show things to. If he likes them, then I know they're good. If he hesitates and says, 'Well, you're not quite done here,' then I know I'm not quite done here." Her two sisters have shared in her process, as well. In *Safekeeping*, Thomas actually includes short conversations with one of her sisters, conversations that turn the lens to examine the actual process of bringing the story to the page. It's like her sister is reading the book along with us, and she occasionally interrupts Thomas to ask for clarification, to question her motives, to make her provide more information. "I couldn't resist," Thomas explains when I ask her about this narrative device. "It was a very important part of the book. It was a way of illuminating things that I couldn't illuminate without my sister. She gave me new ways to think about things. And many of those conversations were just hilarious."

She cautions, though, "I certainly don't show it to a whole bunch of people, because if you get a whole bunch of different reactions before you know what you're doing, then you're sunk."

For both memoirs, Thomas had to write about a hundred pages before the thought that these were indeed books didn't feel quite so terrifying. "It's not exactly an adventure, but it is something you have to get to the end of. You don't know what the end is going to be. It's not so much that you're writing a book but that you are discovering stuff that has a beginning, and what the end is, you have no idea until you realize where you want to get to. And then you have to earn it. So it's really not so much about writing a book as it is writing to the end. And then if it's a book, great!"

Out my car window, I watch a sparrow perched on the wrought-iron fence next to the road, a twig clenched in its beak. It flits its head from side to side and seems to be contemplating its next move. I ask Thomas, "So how did you get to the point where you could say, 'This is the ending'?"

She refers to one poignant conversation with Rogin that became the closing chapter of *A Three Dog Life*—a rare moment of clarity when he talks to her about the pieces of his accident that he remembers. She writes, "I ask Rich if he knows how long we've been married. 'About a year,' he answers. I shake my head. 'Seventeen years,' I say, 'we got married in 1988 and it's 2005.' 'Abby,' he says, smiling, 'our life has been so easy that the days glide by.'"

Thomas makes it a habit to carry her notebook with her all the time, and having it close by was particularly important to her in the years following Rogin's accident. "He said these wonderful things, and I was afraid that if I didn't write them down, I might forget." Of this specific conversation she says, "It was five years into the whole awful experience when Rich and I had that conversation, and it was long before I was through with the book," she tells me. "I don't think I knew when I was writing it down, but it was where I wanted to get to. I knew it when I was putting the piece together. That was what I wanted the ending to be. I don't really know why. There was that one single time when he talked about the accident, and I thought, my God, he's going back to a place that I want to get past. This is kind of a miraculous moment that crystallized the whole experience."

"Did you ever question whether you should write about these experiences or parts of these experiences?"

"No, not really," Thomas responds. "I was careful not to do an injury." In some particular cases, this meant not writing about the people who could potentially be injured. She chuckles. "They simply don't appear."

Thomas believes that the writer has to function with a certain level of ruthlessness—that the story must come first. "It was a question of what had to be written. But you can only do it from your point of view. There are some things that have to go in, but you have to look at your motive. If this is some sort of revenge or if you've got a motive that isn't clear, and if it isn't just exactly what absolutely needs to be in the book, then you leave it alone." Her words remind me of Andre Dubus's conversation with Richard Russo when he was trying to decide how to write about his family. "You really don't need to hurt anybody," Thomas says. "The person you are exposing is yourself. That's the adventure you're taking. That's the search you are on."

Finishing each memoir felt great for Thomas. "There was a relief to feeling that I'd gotten the whole thing," she explains. "It's like when you are very pregnant and you have this huge roundness in front of you. I felt kind of round and full, and I had done it. I'd done what I set out or didn't know I'd set out to do. I had done something sort of beyond what I could have imagined because I'd never taken that trip before."

Both finished books gave Thomas an immense sense of satisfaction. "It wasn't so much a weight off my person, but I think we all need a way to express or make something out of experiences that otherwise have no meaning. If what you want is clarity and meaning, you have to break the secrets over your knee and make something of those ingredients." There's unmistakable pride in her voice when she adds, "I'd made something that meant nothing mean something."

These same words in some way thread through every conversation I've had since starting this project. Meaning emerges when we invest in writing and shaping our stories.

Thomas says candidly that it really would have been enough for the stories to only mean something to her. The critical praise that both books received, though, demonstrates that what meant something to her has also meant something to a lot of other people too. In 2006, *A Three Dog Life* was named a best book of the year by both the *Los Angeles Times* and the *Washington Post*.

For Thomas, though, the personal responses are the ones that have meant the most. "I had no idea what reader response would be," she admits. "The nicest thing anybody has ever said to me came from a woman who'd read *A Three Dog Life*." The woman's husband had suffered a traumatic brain injury too. "She said, 'I used to feel so guilty, and now I just feel human.' And I wanted just that reaction from readers because that happened for me. Guilt is such a crippling and pointless place to live." Thomas sighs. Even over the phone, I can hear the quiet shift in her tone as she remembers this interaction. "I don't think you can ask for any better response from a reader than that."

Thomas is validated by this kind of response to her work. "It's a reason to be honest in a way that's uncomfortable. To discover things about yourself that you wish weren't true." She recognizes the universality in the ways people connect to her loss despite the diversity of circumstances. "There are so many experiences where the details are different but the feelings are the same. I've been enormously grateful to those who have seen themselves in my stories."

Thomas has also accepted that she relinquishes her ability to regulate how people respond to her story once it's out of her hands. "I have control over how I present it, but I have no control over people's responses. And," she adds, "I don't actually give a shit. Of course, I'm really happy when the books are helpful in one way or another, but if they are not, well, so be it." She laughs and says, "Plenty of people have complained that *A Three Dog Life* hardly has any dogs in it! But that's their prerogative."

Thomas is not quite as secure in these feelings when reflecting on her forthcoming memoir, *What Comes Next and How to Like It*, a book about growing older, enduring life's uncertain twists and turns, and seeing the beauty amidst it all. "I'm a little less sure of it," she confesses, "but it's coming out anyway." When the book is published, in early 2015, to a stunning array of rave reviews, Thomas will discover that she had nothing to worry about.

Thomas says that the thing that has surprised her the most about the experience of writing and sharing her stories is "how much easier it is to look at what you're hiding from than to keep it in the basement. It's much scarier, has much more power in the dark than brought up to the light."

She continues, "Once what was in the basement began to have a shape so I could grab it, I just had to do that. And it is much diminished in the light. You know those moments in scary movies when you don't know what's coming? It's so much less scary when the thing is actually there. Then it's just a finite thing. But the fear about it and the guilt about it and the everything else, when it's in the dark, is infinite."

I admit to Thomas that there are still many things connected to my story that I'm afraid of and have yet to grab from the dark of my basement. "Is this knowledge that it's scarier in the dark, that I'll survive bringing it into the light, something that I can only discover by doing it myself?" I ask.

"Yes," she responds. "But you are not going to survive it if you don't do it. You know you have this place you need to go. If you don't go there, it will rule you forever."

Thomas reflects on her experience of going to the places she needed to go through her writing. "In a funny way, this puts it in the past—although it is probably always going to be alive—but you will have made something out of it. It's so important to make something of it that isn't exactly what the story was." She sighs, and I wonder if she is sometimes still weighed down by what her stories once were before she made something different out of them. "You've survived the experience, now make something of it."

Thomas has subtly shifted the conversation away from her work and is now focused on mine. "I'm sure you are going to do this, Melanie, because you don't have a choice. You are a writer. This is what you are writing," she says. "You really don't have a choice," she repeats.

"I feel like I've stepped out on the tightrope and I'm too far to turn back, but I have no idea how close I am to the other side," I confess.

"Both feet on the wire," Thomas encourages. "At some point you'll figure out where you are headed. A memoir is how I got here from there. You have to decide where the here is."

I like the way she puts it. It's up to me to decide. Maybe "here" is only a few more steps along the wire. I know I have to face my fear; I have to start grabbing those things from my dark basement, if I'm ever going to find out.

I also know that when I do, I will hold Thomas's last words before we say our good-byes like a flashlight to help illuminate my way: "Don't forget," she insists, her voice alive with the wisdom of her experience, "it's scarier not to do it than to do it."

CHAPTER 9

Monica Wood

*· When We Were the Kennedys:
A Memoir from Mexico, Maine*

As I drive north on I-95 toward Portland, Maine, to meet author Monica Wood on a Thursday in late March 2014, I flip to the public broadcasting station on the radio. In a chance moment of synchronicity, the program is the "Maine Calling Book Club," and the chosen book is *When We Were the Kennedys*, by Monica Wood. This award-winning memoir is a richly woven story set in the 1960s company mill town of Mexico, Maine, that seamlessly threads Wood's family's grief following her father's sudden death with the decline of the town's paper mill and the national tragedy of the Kennedy assassination. For the next hour, I listen to the host and her three guests discuss the story, the sliver of history it renders, and the resonance the book has had for readers. A call-in segment follows, and I am intrigued by how many of the callers begin with a nominal reference to something in Wood's book, but then turn the lens on their own stories. Some compare their childhoods in different mill towns to Wood's; others expound on their views of unions or their experiences in Catholic schools. One caller launches right into her own lengthy story about growing up in Chisolm, Maine, without even mentioning Wood's book. The host interrupts her at one point with a not-so-subtle nudge: "And, so, you can relate to Monica Wood's story, then?"

"This is just what people do," Wood says later as we sit in a back booth of Shay's Pub, a relaxed neighborhood grill tucked in Portland's Monument Square area, and share a decadent piece of chocolate lava cake. "You can find it either annoying or endearing. If you choose to find it endearing, then you have to think, well, this is what happens with a book. You meet somebody halfway, and the book becomes something other than what you wrote. If a hundred thousand people read your book, it means that you've written a hundred thousand books, because it's different for every single person. But take it as a compliment that people see something of themselves in your writing. You've touched something very deep in them."

Wood's timeless beauty and natural grace make her appear considerably younger than her almost sixty-one years. Her red hair is cut in a smart pixie style. She has a sparkling smile that spreads to her eyes. Earlier that week, I'd e-mailed a writer friend who knows Wood and said I was a little nervous about our meeting. He responded: "Monica will be hugging you and knitting you socks while you interview her." I discover within the first thirty seconds what he meant. Wood is a lovely person. She's genuine and sincere, and any nervousness I feel dissipates as we begin our conversation about her journey to write *When We Were the Kennedys*.

Wood's effortless ability to put people at ease in this way is what draws readers to her writing. Her literary voice reflects the same sincerity I encounter in her person, and when I read her memoir, she guided me through the heartbreak of her family story with a gentle and compassionate hand.

So I'm surprised to learn that *When We Were the Kennedys* is Wood's first real venture into memoir writing. "I had never really written any memoir at all. Even my fiction wasn't very autobiographical."

The memoir journey began when Wood was asked to contribute an essay to an anthology, *A Place Called Maine*, published in 2008, about what it is like to live and write in Maine. The editor, then Maine poet laureate Wes McNair, asked her to write a piece about growing up in the town of Mexico. "[Writing this] was kind of foreign territory, and I didn't really want to do it, to tell you the truth. It wasn't something that I had bottled up that I was dying to tell, but he's a hard guy to say no to, so I said yes, but I really didn't know where to start." The story felt overwhelming in its complexity. "How do you write about something so big, which is about growing up in a community like that at that time?" she'd asked.

Wood somehow needed to zoom in on one aspect of her experience. And the day her father died is the defining moment that comes to mind whenever she goes back to her childhood.

On a crisp April morning in 1963, a morning like any other morning for nine-year-old Wood, her beloved father left their third-floor apartment, lunch pail in hand, and headed to the Oxford Paper Company, a few blocks away, where he worked as a foreman. He never made it. On the way, he suffered a massive heart attack and died. Wood and the rest of her family—three sisters, a brother, and their mother—reeled in the wake of this staggering loss, and her world was redefined by this singular event.

"So, I thought, I'll just write about that day and see if I can get at something larger through this small lens," Wood explains. That "something larger" became *When We Were the Kennedys*. The memoir's prologue and first chapter are variations on the essay Wood wrote for the anthology.

Things didn't just click and fall into place at that point, though. It was a couple of years later, when Wood found herself in what she calls "a place of utter writerly despair," that she tried another one of these autobiographical essays. She wrote about her older sister, Anne, and saw a connection between this piece and her other essay about Mexico. "I realized I was writing something a lot bigger." The story was in there somewhere, she knew, but she had to do some significant digging. "I started writing down scenes, jotting down things that I thought would belong in a book like this." She laughs. "It was just kind of bumping into my nose for a while."

Wood thought the story would be about one main thing: how her father's death reshaped her family. "Kind of the before and after; this family and then that family." But something shifted as she began writing. "There's a certain magic at work when a book is really meant to be born." Enthusiasm brightens her voice. "It's so hard to describe now, but I just remember that all these little details would fit so perfectly, thematically and metaphorically and every other way."

Mexico's paper mill quickly became a main character in the book. "You can't write about anything in that town without the mill being a part of it." The mill's ever-presence becomes for Wood a metaphor for God in a way: "It giveth and taketh," she says. The mill's influence also revealed the importance of the historical context and how President John F. Kennedy's assassination played a role in her story.

"I think of memoir as nesting dolls," Wood muses. "For me, the big one was the country—the times, the era, the assassination. Then inside that, the company town, the mill, management beginning its long decline. And then, inside that is the family and their loss."

By the end of a year of writing, Wood had a "sort-of draft" of the book. "It was very, very expository." Her tone is one of disdain and she makes a face before sighing. "It was not very good."

Wood put the sort-of draft away and began again. "I just started taking out all of the exposition and putting everything into scene. I think that was when I decided I wanted it to be a book." She was reluctant writing those scenes, though, and felt paranoid about fiddling around with the truth. "I hate memoirs where I can just smell it on the first page, and I say, 'Well I know that didn't happen. What a coincidence.' But it is true that some things are stranger than fiction." She gestures to a copy of her book resting on the edge of the table. "There are things in there that I'm sure people think I made up that are the bone truth." Wood was even hesitant to do things like think as someone else or write dialogue.

These fears make sense to me. She was, after all, writing from her perspective as a nine-year-old girl almost fifty years later. Memories, especially childhood ones, are subjective. I tell Wood about a scene I've just written that's been bothering me because I feel like maybe I've created a mash-up of more than one conversation.

"I want to say not to be afraid to put memories together," she urges. "That was a real hurdle I had, because I really wanted the memoir to be true. Honest. Some of the scenes I've put together are like little chips. Remember those cheap kaleidoscopes we used to get? They're like little sequins of memory that kind of fall into a certain place."

A moment of revelation came when Wood received an e-mail from a neighbor who'd lived on the block where her father died. "He wrote, 'You know I lived on the third floor and I remember seeing your father that morning.' He described him and said he remembered seeing him with his hat off his head."

Wood had written that scene only through the lens of her imagination. "I had no idea what my father looked like when he was found. I know he fell. I know he hit his head. And I know he was lying on the ground and that's how people saw him. So I added in my memory of how I thought it looked—his lunch pail was here and his cap was knocked off his head." Wood's vision of that morning had become her former neighbor's own fifty-year-old memory, even though he'd witnessed the scene firsthand. "I thought, my God, I'm altering people's memory!"

She continues, "What you are trying to get to is the truth of your experience, which isn't the same as the truth of the truth, because there isn't any such thing."

Wood began to understand that the tools she relies on to write fiction, her chosen genre, could help her with the memoir. These tools had already served her very well: she'd written four novels,

MONICA WOOD · 105

including *My Only Story*—a finalist for the Kate Chopin Literary Award—and numerous anthologized short stories, among them, a 1999 Pushcart Prize winner.

So Wood approached her story like she would a novel: "scene to scene to scene," she says. "And I decided to tell it chronologically. Chronology is your best friend when you're writing a memoir. Even if it feels like a false structure, you need something, if only so you don't go insane writing this." In Wood's case, chronology gave her a scaffold and led to the breakthrough in the process that she really needed.

Wood's changed approach helped her to make sense of how her personal story connected to the larger picture. "Once the idea of the mill strike became the beating heart of the chronology, I started pulling in more memories about that as a way of looking at the whole thing. The art of memoir is really so much about what you leave out. There are a million stories that you are going to leave on the wayside, really important ones, for the sake of the bigger story you want to tell."

Wood's next statement catches me off guard. "What surprised me the most was how much fun it was process-wise, once I figured out how similar it was to writing a novel. I've just never had more joy writing anything."

Wood's use of the word "joy" to describe writing about her family's grief in the wake of her father's untimely death is unexpected. "Joyful" is not the way most of the memoir writers I've talked to characterize the process of telling their hard stories. "Joyful" is certainly not the way I characterize telling my hard story.

"Can you help me understand where the joy came from?" I ask.

"Partly it was the narrative problem before me that I figured out exactly the right way to solve. I loved that." Of the subject matter, she says, "I was looking back and it was almost like I was writing about this little girl that I knew really, really well, but I could separate myself from her and her family. They began to feel like fictional characters to me in a very fond way."

Wood acknowledges that this response might be unusual. "It was a funny experience because it is a painful story in many parts, and those parts were very hard to write, but I never cried." She pauses, her expression thoughtful as she further reflects on her reaction to the writing, and then adds, "There was a lot of light in my life even during that dark time."

In Wood's memoir, she vividly portrays some wonderful individuals who helped her to survive her loss: Father Bob, her gentle and flawed uncle. The Vaillancourts, a family who welcomes a heartbroken girl into their home, recognizing her need for something whole. Her sister Anne, the undisputed saint in this story, whose generosity and selflessness hold her family together. It makes sense that there would be joy for Wood in writing about these very kind people.

I am relieved to hear that though Wood didn't experience the same difficult emotions I'm facing in writing my family story, she does understand them. "The original conception for my book was that the two bookends were going to be my father's death and my mother's death ten years later. I went through the whole draft absolutely terrified to get to my mother because I did not want to write about her death."

Wood admits that had she followed that concept and written a memoir about her adult life, something she vows now never to do, the experience would have been markedly different. The narrative of her mother's death would not have the "cloak of childhood innocence" that enveloped *When We Were the Kennedys*. "I couldn't do it. Too much guilt, too much . . ." Her sentence trails off, but its implications are clear. Hard stories take us through hard territory.

"I also would feel that I was treading on my siblings' story," Wood continues.

While she was writing her memoir, Wood didn't consult with her sisters or brother about their family's history. "This one I kept pretty close to the vest. I deliberately didn't ask them anything. I wanted it to be my memory." But when she finished the manuscript, her siblings were among Wood's first readers.

I'd heard from a number of the other authors I interviewed that they were intentional about *not* sharing the finished work with their families before publication because they didn't want anyone dictating what should or shouldn't be in there. "What made you decide that you needed to share the draft with your family?" I ask Wood.

"These people did not ask to be in my story. I feel like if they were writing a memoir, I would certainly want to see what they wrote before it came out and have the chance to say what feels like an invasion of my privacy." She qualifies, "My sibs love me and really respect me as an artist."

For Wood, finishing the book did not have a particularly cathartic feel because she hadn't written it with a burning need to purge the experience. The book was a story she'd wanted to tell, and she felt good about the way she'd done it.

The greater and unanticipated satisfaction for Wood came from the reader response after the memoir's publication. "I expected nothing. I really mean it. Nothing." She didn't think anyone would be interested in publishing it. And even after she'd sold it, she didn't think anyone outside western Maine would be interested in reading it. "I was completely wrong. The most surprising part is just how universal it turned out to be. So many people said, 'I love this. I'm so glad you wrote it. I'm so glad you've shown what it was like.' It's just a unique book in the sense that it's revealing a way of life that many people don't know anything about. You know those little towns that we go through and we never even look."

I consider the radio show I listened to on my drive and the callers who seemed compelled to connect their own experiences to Wood's. They are no different from me. The whole reason I'm sitting across from Wood sharing cake in this pub is because I found chips of my story in hers and her words reverberate at some level in me.

"You know, our species wants to connect," Wood reflects. "We're pack animals. And people are just so endlessly kind."

Wood's story embodies this universal connection. At nine years old, grieving the loss of her father, she also identifies with an entire nation grieving the loss of President Kennedy. That connection makes her feel less alone.

"This is the voice I want you to hear when you are feeling in despair about your own book," Wood tells me now. "What I've discovered about memoirs and the reason people love them is that every family story in one way or another is everybody's family story."

Isolation is at the core of my family story. Embedded somewhere in Wood's discovery is the possibility that sharing my family story could break it free from that isolation. Maybe sharing it will allow me to reach out to the pack and grasp a kind hand. A kind hand like the one Monica Wood has been extending since our conversation began. Wood's encouraging smile stretches across the table, and her optimism and warmth feel like that hug my writer friend predicted.

CHAPTER 10

Mark Doty

· *Heaven's Coast*

George drops the tattered tennis ball a few inches from my feet and sets his expectant gaze on me. I bend over, pick up the ball, and toss it down the grass-tufted dirt path ahead. George charges after it, floppy ears bobbing, and wrestles the ball to a stop. He trots back, shaking it to the death, and sets it like a prize at my feet again. Bedlington terriers were originally bred as vermin killers, so it's only natural for George to see his task as more than simple ball retrieval. I throw it once more and laugh as Ned, a bulky, loveable golden retriever, emerges from his explorations of the overgrown bushes that line the path and joins in the chase.

"This is really beautiful," I say to poet and author Mark Doty as we amble behind his dogs. Though fog shrouded the Cross Sound ferry on my early crossing from New London, Connecticut, to Orient Point, New York, and wind-swept swells made my stomach churn in the enclosed cabin, forcing me out onto the misty deck, a warm midday sun has since burned off the clouds. It's turned into a gorgeous day.

Springs Dog Park in East Hampton, New York, is touted as one of the largest fenced-in dog parks in the country with its twenty-plus acres of trails and open, grassy fields. Just down the road from where Jackson Pollock's studio barn sits, its floors spattered still with evidence of his creativity, and a few miles from Doty's charming weekend-retreat home, it's a pristine and appropriate backdrop for us to begin our conversation about his memoir work. Dogs, after all, have been sources of steadfast comfort for Doty as he's journeyed through moments of profound grief.

Doty's most recent memoir, *Dog Years*, published in 2008, offers an intimate glimpse into the relationship he had with the two dogs, Beau and Arden, he credits with keeping him alive when the darkness of loss threatened to swallow him whole.

We've only just met, but there's something comfortably familiar about this tall, handsome, sixty-year-old man strolling at my side, head bald, his gray goatee trimmed close. Maybe that familiarity is a natural offshoot of reading someone's memoir, but with Doty, I suspect it's more. We share some strikingly common ground.

Doty's partner of twelve years, Wally Roberts, died of a viral brain infection called progressive multifocal leukoencephalopathy, PML, which can affect people with AIDS. That was in January 1994, less than two years before my father died of pneumocystis pneumonia, PCP, another AIDS-related illness. Though the circumstances of our stories and our losses are distinct, our journeys took us at the same time, down the same road paved by an epidemic riddled with acronyms that Doty fittingly calls, "A bad hand drawn at Scrabble, letters which we can figure and refigure and still make nothing," in his award-winning memoir, *Heaven's Coast*.

I'm here to talk about the genesis of that book, so stunning in its raw portrayal of grief, so moving in its loving depiction of a deeply valued life, so beautiful in its lyrical approach to the realities of illness and death and all that comes after. Doty began writing the memoir almost immediately following Roberts's death, at a time when, he says frankly, "I had no idea if I was going to be okay."

Doty and Roberts had lived with the reality of AIDS for five years before Roberts's death. In that time, they'd watched this disease in all its cruelty steal the lives of so many of their friends and acquaintances. They'd felt it slowly stealing their own lives as Roberts's health deteriorated in the last two years of his life. But nothing prepared Doty for what he describes in *Heaven's Coast* as "an absence so forceful it is itself a daily, hourly presence."

"So what made you start writing about it?" I ask as we walk through the park, continuing the fetch game with George and Ned.

Doty says that in the wake of Roberts's death, he felt "immobilized." He couldn't read. Couldn't concentrate. "It's a common thing in that kind of state of new grief," he theorizes. "It's like you've been atomized." While living in that state, Doty felt a magnetic pull to the natural world. He had grant money that allowed him to take some time for himself. His home then was in Provincetown, Massachusetts, and the town was surrounded by a beautiful preservation space of sand dunes, forests, and ponds. "Walking the dogs in those days was my chief occupation, and that became a way to think and feel," he explains.

Doty had already forged a prominent writing career by that time. He'd published three collections of poetry. The third book, *My Alexandria*, won the National Book Critics Circle Award and the *Los Angeles Times* Book Prize. In 1993, when the collection was published in the United Kingdom, Doty won the prestigious T. S. Eliot Prize, becoming the first American poet to receive the honor.

Two months before Roberts's death, when Roberts was very sick, Doty received an invitation to contribute an essay to a book called *Wrestling with the Angel: Gay Men Write About Faith and Religion*. Too immersed in Roberts's daily care at the time, Doty had put all thoughts of the essay on the back shelf. But about three weeks after Roberts died, Doty thought of a sentence that might be an interesting opener to the piece. Then he thought about what words might follow that sentence. "I thought, if you're thinking like this, you should try it." He started writing.

"It felt like such a gift and a relief for me to just focus and be still with a clear path in which to think, because that had just not been available to me." He wrote that essay and almost immediately began another one. And another one after that. He'd take the dogs walking in a "sort of meditative state" he recalls. "So writing about that was useful too, because it was a way to reflect on the reflection and also gave some form to the reflection."

Doty wasn't thinking of a book when he began. In a theme I'd come to hear echoed by other writers who wrote while they journeyed through their hard experiences, he says the writing was primarily a way for him to cope. Gradually, though, he began to recognize a connective theme in the essays he'd written. "These seemed to be part of a continuous unfolding—what it is like to be in new grief, witnessing it, really paying attention to that state to see what I could learn from it and primarily how I could get through it." He began to recognize something else as the writing unfolded. "There was a notion in the back of my mind that [the writing] might potentially have some use for readers. There weren't so many books that were not written from a distance of time or from a kind of 'self-help' perspective. There were all of these books that wanted to tell you that what you are experiencing is normal, and you'll be okay." What Doty was in the midst of experiencing was to him "a normal that was extraordinary, heartbreaking, and unbearable." Perhaps people would want to read about that.

"When you recognized that it was a book, did it change your approach?" I ask.

Doty found comfort in not having to know exactly where he was headed in the writing. "If you are writing a book, it means that questions that are posed here can be reexamined later. An image that has a certain value or meaning in this piece might look different later on. There's space for that," Doty explains. "That means that you don't have to arrive at so much closure. It lets you slow down in the sense that there's time."

Though Doty is first a poet, writing prose was not new to him. He'd written reviews and essays. But this was the first time he'd ever ventured into writing anything so personal or so lengthy in a prose form. "I was doing something I didn't know how to do; I felt like a real novice with my first prose book, and I felt that it was crucial for me to do it, but in terms of shaping something like that for the reader, I felt really, rawly inexperienced."

His outlook changed at a poetry reading in New York when he met Robert Jones, an editor at HarperCollins. During their conversation, Jones asked Doty about his current writing, and Doty told him about the new track he was on. Later, Doty sent him the essays he'd written, and Jones liked them. "He got them," he adds. Jones also understood the challenges Doty faced with the shift away from poetry, where the chief characteristic is compression, to prose, where there's a lot more space to move around. "I wanted to expand, spread out, but I also needed some help in knowing when I'd gone too far with that, or when the book was losing its rudder, which is inevitable some of the time. So Robert was there and ready to do those things. I felt like I had someone to catch it as I was doing it."

This idea of needing somebody to "catch" your work implies an innate precariousness involved in the process of producing it. A fragility to the words emerging on the page. Doty expresses the value in finding the right people to help you take care of them.

Doty and I settle on a park bench and watch the dogs play in the open field. Ned seems to have taken a special liking to me, and he props his front paws on my lap. I rub his neck. For Doty, one of the most encouraging parts of his involvement with Jones was that Jones did not try to interfere with the structural design of the book itself. "This actually surprised me," Doty says, "because I think it's very eccentric." There is a unique quality to the memoir's shape. It begins immediately after Roberts's death and goes through several months of walking, thinking, reading, and talking about the aftermath of the loss with only little bits of the story's past. And then it essentially stops and restarts, telling about how Doty and Roberts met, details about their life together, and then the full story of Roberts's illness and death.

"It's an odd structure," Doty admits, "but one that felt true to the composing process. And I wanted process to be part of the text, to be written into the text, because it's really a book about the wrestling with a person's disappearance and what do we go through in trying to shape the story of that. Shaping the story is one of the things that will keep you alive."

Along with the structural shift that happens midway through *Heaven's Coast*, a distinctive transition also occurs in the book's style and tone. In the first section, there's a sort of glow to the language—an elegy-like beauty as Doty describes the range of emotions that fill him as he explores this mysterious and sometimes even radiant world of grief. But then, in the second section, when he starts back at the beginning of his relationship with Roberts, things change. Doty writes, "Much as I want to hold on, want to cling to any perception which might be redemptive, any solid point, what is required of me is what I fear the most: relinquishment, free fall, the fluid pour into absolute emptiness. There is no way around the emptiness, the bitter fact, no way to go but *through*." The remainder of the book is an in-depth journey from the moment of diagnosis to the moment of Roberts's death. The writing is stark and real, and it does not gloss over the brutality of this disease. I ask Doty to tell me more about this change in approach.

"I did feel initially that I could write this book that would be stepping through the world in the raw but indeed beautiful light of Wally's dying. I think because he died at home, and I was so close to it, that when he left his body, I felt in some ways a piece of me went with him. That upward pull was so clear to me, in the sense of everything having a kind of strange shine to it. And then the understanding dawns that I've seen the light, but he's still not here, and writing this does not bring him back. No one gets to stay in that state of elevation. It's just not human to stay. So you come back. You come crashing back to the world, because he's just plain gone."

A significant catalyst that brought Doty crashing back to the world was the tragic death of his beloved friend and colleague poet

Lynda Hull. She was killed in a single-car accident two months after Roberts died. "Her death was not attended by any of that same sort of shine that I'd felt after Wally's death. We don't know what condition she was in when she died, but it was part of a yearlong crashing and burning. Hers just felt like a loss in which it was impossible to make any meaning. It was just so awful. Dismal. Here was a wonderful poet, and dear friend, and the most amazing and insightful person. Such incredible strength as an artist. And she was just . . ." Doty stops and swallows hard. "Gone." The rug got pulled out from under him, and all the radiant light he'd felt in the immediate wake of Roberts's dying vanished, and all he felt was the full despair of his absence.

Writing about that kind of despair was the most difficult thing for him to do, but he was determined to keep going. "There was the momentum that had already been established—a sense of no matter what's going on, I'm the witness here, so this practice that had become pretty much daily kept me working."

Reentering some of the most wrenching moments, especially the scene of Roberts's actual death, was by far the hardest. "It was like just pushing my way up this very tall, spirally staircase. I'd write and cry and write and cry and write and cry," he says. "But I also felt exhilarated by its completion. I had done something that was really important to me, which was giving a form to that year." He pauses and looks across the field. When he meets my gaze again, his eyes are tear-filled, and I feel my own eyes stinging. "I felt like in that book, like I had made something that stands where Wally and I were." His voice catches on the emotion of the memory before he says, "And that's the best we could do."

We walk along the remainder of the path and circle back to his car with the dogs running ahead. We return to Doty's quaint, cottage-style shingled house and continue our conversation about *Heaven's Coast* and Wally Roberts and grief and survival there. We sit in a backyard garden on a stone patio, panting dogs flanking us, and overlook a walled fishpond where Doty's partner, Alex Hadel, clad in hip-high waders, dredges muck and weeds from its bottom.

I scratch behind Ned's ears and ask whether Doty ever feared that making his story public might diminish it.

"There was a particularly loathsome British reviewer—there they take the gloves off," he qualifies, "and this guy called me 'a cannibal feasting off of [my] lover's body.'" I gasp at the cruelty of such a statement. Doty sighs, visibly still disturbed by the reviewer's words. "It was just awful, but he's also probably a person who really dislikes the form. Some people have some real chips on their shoulder about memoir." It's true that memoir was still gaining traction as a legitimate literary genre in 1994 when Doty published *Heaven's Coast*.

Doty emphasizes that writers of memoir can't be hindered by criticism like this one reviewer's. For him, the nature of the genre is translating our own perceptions into language. "Other people's subjectivity is not a part of it," he explains.

Doty does confess to encountering some initial moments of regret after writing the book. "When I was on book tour, I had an awful episode of believing that I had substituted the book for my life, for my memories," he says. "That the story that I had made was the story and even that I would forget what was done in it." But then he had a very vivid memory of a time in his life with Roberts that he hadn't written into the book. Discovering that he still carried those kinds of private moments eased any of that anxiety. "I was so grateful for them. Memory was capacious—always yielding more. Life was larger than the book."

The critical response to *Heaven's Coast* has been overwhelmingly positive, earning Doty the PEN/Martha Albrand Award for First Nonfiction in 1997. In the twenty years since its publication, the book has connected to countless readers and opened the door for them to hold up their own stories of loss, of pain, of illness, of grief. "It was a vehicle for the feelings of others."

What Doty hadn't expected when he wrote *Heaven's Coast* was how people whose particulars were so different from his own would really find themselves in the book. "These letters would say, 'I could so relate to your story, I felt just like you did, and I can't thank you enough. Here's what happened to me.' But the story would be about a son who died in a motorcycle accident or losing a parent to Alzheimer's. There was a letter from a guy who could not go home because his country no longer existed; there was no nation to return to. And so all of these experiences of loss, although they bore individual characteristics, were basically the same experience."

As with almost all the writers I have met on this journey, the greatest reward of the process for Doty is knowing that his story has made a difference to others. "This is exactly what I wanted to happen. You make a kind of emotional connection that is quite profound, and people make use of what you have done. It's nice to get a compliment or have your writing praised, but when somebody can say, 'Your book showed me this,' or 'This is what I got from it,' that's what I love the most." He describes hearing stories of how people would read the book to their loved ones who were sick or how people read parts of it at memorial services. "People were doing amazing things with it," he says. "The University of St. Thomas, which is in Minneapolis, used it as a common text for the freshman class. And I thought, this is just incredible. Thirteen hundred *Catholic* freshmen in the Midwest are talking about this book!" He chuckles at the obvious irony, considering the Catholic Church's stance on homosexuality. "This is heaven in a way, because it's an antidote to isolation. It makes one feel less alone in the world."

Doty adds a beautiful image to the narrative. With a catch in his voice that pulls at my emotional core, he describes a transcendent moment when he heard Roberts's voice declare, "Look at all these friends I have now."

As if sensing the intimacy of the conversation, Ned stands up from where he's been lying on the patio and nudges against my leg. Then, he places his large front paws squarely on my thighs, pulls up on his hind legs, and brings his gentle face close to mine. He gives a combination of a whine and a growl, a clear message that he wants me to pat him. I stroke his neck and he leans into my hand. "He's a dog that's all feeling," Doty says with a laugh. "The barometer is so sensitive, you know?" A poet, too, I think.

As our conversation wraps up, I throw in a final question. The most important one: "Did writing the book lessen the burden of your grief?"

Doty doesn't respond right away, and I sense he's weighing his answer. "The experience is so not over," he finally says. "Whatever a book might do to make you feel like you have laid something to rest, you're not finished with it. I don't mean I have to write the story again, but you go on living the story. A rupture in your life of that kind remains a hole, a tear. Despite the fact that it doesn't repair, doesn't make that rupture in your life go away, it's a very satisfying thing to do to give shape to your story. To concretize it. To have something you can give people and say, 'I made this. This stands for me.' It's a joy."

He offers me a heartening promise: "And when you are done with your memoir, you'll want to write another one. And so there is a life ahead of you of telling other stories."

In the comfortable silence that follows, I absorb the beauty of the garden. Budding perennials surround the space where we sit, and as a non-gardener, I can only imagine the work and effort that goes into creating such an intricate and appealing landscape. What I do understand, though, is that in the same way it does every spring, new life is about to blossom all around us.

Ned flops down on the ground between our chairs, and Doty rests a hand on the dog's head. "I didn't want to forget Wally. I didn't want to just move on. I have not been immobilized by grief, but I have certainly carried it with me." His gaze settles on Hadel, knee-deep in the pond, his back to us, long, muck-laced weeds clutched in his hands. A year and a half from now, following the Supreme Court's decision to legalize gay marriage nationwide, the two will marry.

After a long pause, Doty quietly adds, "I have continued to have a life."

CHAPTER 11

Edwidge Danticat

· *Brother, I'm Dying*

The Hospitality Lounge at the Miami Book Fair is definitely *the* place to be. There's an endless buffet of free food, a great coffee barista, and, more important, a revolving door of some of the most notable literary voices of our time moving through the space at any given moment. For the second day in a row, as a guest of my editor, the director of Beacon Press, Helene Atwan, I'm moving among them. A new and unknown writer working on her first book, I feel like an imposter. And I have to admit that it's been hard to keep my personal awe in check at seeing some of my writing heroes—Sandra Cisneros, Amy Hempel, Nick Flynn, Mary Karr, Sven Birkerts—chatting nearby. A moment ago, I stood close enough to Joyce Carol Oates that I could have reached out and touched her. I didn't, but I could have.

For the thirty-second year, the international book festival has descended on the Wolfson campus of Miami Dade College in downtown Miami. The sun and warmth of the last two days have been welcome reprieves from the plummeting temperatures that late November has ushered in at home in New Hampshire. I've relished the luxury of sitting in on some excellent readings and panels and wandering around the book vendor booths of the Street Fair. The night before, tagging along with Atwan to the weekend author party, I even got to witness the musical phenomenon known as "The Rock Bottom Remainders"—a band comprising best-selling authors, including Amy Tan, Mitch Albom, Dave Barry, and Scott Turow, who are admittedly better writers than they are stellar musicians.

All these things are secondary to my real purpose for being in Miami. This morning, I'm meeting with award-winning author Edwidge Danticat for a conversation about her exquisite and heartbreaking memoir, *Brother, I'm Dying*, an intimate family story of love and death and new life, and a powerful witness to the large-scale injustices so many immigrants face upon entering this country.

It's a full weekend for Danticat. I met her briefly the day before when we walked together between two venues while she rapidly switched gears from participating in a poignant panel discussion about her writing for a book of photographs and essays called *Havana and Haiti: Two Cultures, One Community* to presenting a reading of her new children's book, *Mama's Nightingale*, to a raucous group of kids under a tent in the area of the festival known as "Children's Alley." After our conversation today, Danticat has a television interview with PBS's *Book View Now*, and later this afternoon, she'll be hosting a discussion and Q&A with actor and writer Sonia Manzano of *Sesame Street* fame about Manzano's new memoir, *Becoming Maria*. I'm grateful Danticat found time for me in the midst of all the action.

Elegant in a black dress and short, white jacket patterned with smoky brushstrokes, Danticat arrives in the hotel lounge, her family in tow. Her husband, Fedo Boyer, greets the surge of people who crowd in to speak to them with an easygoing smile and vigorous handshakes. Their two daughters, ten-year-old Mira and six-year-old Leila, hang back a little, overwhelmed by the attention. Leila clutches a purse, the carrier for her stuffed cat. "Tabitha," she informs me shyly when I ask its name.

Unruffled by all of the attention, Danticat extracts herself from her entourage and guides her family to the line for the buffet. "I figured it would be the best way to get everybody fed with everything else going on today," she confesses with a soft laugh, her face opening into a wide smile, as we head upstairs to a quieter area designated for press. We sit down to talk at a high counter along the window beside a row of tall library shelves stacked with hard-backed books on law and criminal justice.

The irony of conversing about Danticat's memoir amidst these books does not escape either of us. Public government documents played a major role in helping Danticat piece together the astounding story she recounts in its pages. *Brother, I'm Dying* retraces the lives of two brothers from Haiti, the two pivotal men in her life—her father, Mira, and her uncle, Joseph—who, despite decades of separation, end up buried side by side in a cemetery in Queens, New York. Writing her book is how Danticat unraveled the tragic string of circumstances that led to this unforeseen outcome.

In 2004, on the day Danticat learns she's pregnant with her first child, she also learns her father is dying from pulmonary fibrosis. As Mira's health deteriorates, so does the political stability in Haiti where his eighty-one-year-old brother still lives. Joseph, with whom Danticat lived for eight years of her childhood when her parents left Haiti to build a life in America, must flee his home to escape a violent rebellion. He seeks asylum in the United States. In a chain of cruel violations of his fundamental rights, which will make international headlines and further solidify Danticat's commitment to advocate for immigrant justice, Joseph is detained by US Customs, imprisoned at the Krome Detention Center (an immigrant facility near Miami), and dies of undiagnosed acute pancreatitis, shackled and alone, after being transferred to a Miami hospital within days of his arrival. Five months later, Danticat's father also dies. She writes of her driving purpose at the end of her memoir's first chapter: "This is an attempt at cohesiveness, and at re-creating a few wondrous and terrible months when their lives and mine intersected in startling ways, forcing me to look forward and back at the same time. I am writing this only because they can't."

"The first time I thought I should write about this," Danticat tells me now, "was when, after my uncle died and his corpse went to the morgue, the people at Krome, where he had been detained, gave us his briefcase. My uncle always had his briefcase; you never really saw him without it. And when he escaped his house in Haiti, during that most turbulent time that ended up in his coming to Miami in the first place, that was what he took with him." Inside, she found items that exemplified the man she considered a second father: His Bible—her uncle was a Baptist minister. His voicebox with batteries—at fifty-five, he'd undergone a radical laryngectomy to remove a cancerous mass from his throat and lost the ability to speak, except with the help of an artificial larynx he held to his neck to amplify his whispers. Scraps of paper with notes scribbled in her uncle's handwriting—in short testimonial statements, he'd documented the sights and sounds of his final days in Haiti. Tucked in with these personal items was the transcript of Joseph's initial interview with an officer from the Bureau of Customs and Border Protection upon his arrival in the United States.

A photograph of Joseph, his face slanted slightly toward the camera, was clipped to the file. "It was the last picture of him," Danticat says. "To me it was so surreal, and I remember when I was reading that document, and I was looking at his face, that's the first time I thought, I have to write about this."

At forty-seven, Danticat is blessed with a full, beautifully unlined face. Her eyes, the color of rich soil, radiate a quiet grace and charm. Gently accented with the music of her Haitian heritage, her lilting voice often resonates with the emotions of her memories. "People say—it's cliché, but it's true—it does feel like a nightmare. We were just given the interview and the corpse and nothing else. And I was trying to figure out how much to tell my father, who was also very ill. When you don't know what happened to someone you love in their final hours, especially when it ends so badly, it's even worse in your mind. So, writing this book really began as a quest to find out what happened to my uncle at the very end and what led to that end."

When her uncle died, Danticat was already a powerful voice for human rights and immigrant issues. As part of her advocacy, she'd worked with Americans for Immigrant Justice, a nonprofit law firm that champions the basic rights of immigrants, and visited with people in detention. "It was really strange when it was my story suddenly," she explains.

The immigration interview transcript with the bold US seal helped Danticat recognize almost immediately that her uncle's story was bigger than simply her family's experience. "I think as writers we do have the practice of seeing experience both from within and without as we're living it; it's just part of what we do. I think that for me, when I saw that piece of paper, it just made it real. It was the first time that it felt like it was a really big experience, something that was happening to my family, but that has also happened to other people and would continue to happen. And I immediately felt this obligation to speak about it, to use this platform and skill that I have as a writer. It was a personal grief, but no longer personal. It was outside of myself . . . my family. There were other people involved. Powerful people. The document kind of sealed it as an actual public experience—as something that has not just happened to me and my family, but something that's happened in the world."

So, Danticat's initial impulse was to write advocacy articles to draw public attention to the human rights violations that her uncle's story exposed. She wrote an op-ed for the *New York Times* titled "A Very Haitian Story." She worked with other journalists to tell Joseph's story. She appeared on *60 Minutes* in a segment called "Detention in America," which revealed both the neglect and poor medical care in the federal prison system.

To understand the full story for herself, though, Danticat began acquiring more documents from the US government and requested access to her uncle's medical records. Americans for

Immigrant Justice filed a lawsuit and urged the Department of Justice to launch an investigation into her uncle's case. "The investigation basically said nothing was done wrong," she explains—an outcome that's impossible to comprehend when you read the details of what happened to her uncle—"but at least there was an investigation, and the investigation gathered a paper trail."

The paper trail enabled Danticat to create a clear time line of the events leading to her uncle's death. Then, her father died. "And I knew I couldn't write about it without involving my father. I know that the book ends with their deaths, but I knew that it would have to start with their journeys—[and] also the journey of how they interact with the next generation, the reality that was forced upon me: my father was on his way out as my daughter was coming in." A few months after her father's death, Danticat visited the cemetery in Queens and stood before carved images of her father's face and her uncle's face on the same gravestone, as her baby daughter slept in the car. "I thought then, that's the end of the story. And that's when I thought there was a book because there was sort of an arc."

The intense grief following these losses pulled Danticat to comb through every moment. "I had to start thinking about the beginning of my dad's dying and the beginning of my uncle's dying, and also the fact that my daughter announced herself on the same day that I learned my father was dying."

Until then, writing memoir had never appealed to Danticat. She wrote primarily fiction, and when she did write nonfiction, she usually wrote essays. "I felt like I had to tell the whole story," she says of her decision to follow the memoir route. "It was the same urgent feeling that I felt looking at those documents the first time. I just felt like, oh I have to write this story. I had to write it for my daughter. I knew I had to write it for the future." She points to my copy of *Brother, I'm Dying*. "I feel like of all my books, this is the one that will mean the most to my family. To my children. To their children. This is my legacy. This is how my children and their children will know what I knew about my family."

Danticat admits that plunging into the actual writing process was the hardest part. "The material was all there. It was sprawling. It was a lot. And in the beginning," she says, laughing, "I wrote it *all*." She was operating under the assumption that if it happened, she had to put it in. "I was dealing with it like an act of documentation. It was my archive. And part of it was also I wanted to relive it. I was invested in the parts where my uncle and my dad were still alive, because it was like a way of spending that time with them. I got to be with them on the page. So it was very indulgent."

She credits her editor, Robin Desser, with helping her to rein things in. "She said, 'Think of the way you write fiction, the way you tell your other stories. Use that sort of pacing. You're still telling a story.' So that's where the benefit of having written fiction came in, because I used some of those same tools. Tools of pacing and structuring and building scene a certain way."

"How did it feel to start building some of those scenes?" I ask, reflecting on the palpable undercurrent of her outrage, grief, and loss I sensed when reading so many of the scenes in her memoir.

"The most difficult moments were actually the moments closest to the present. There's so much guilt involved, maybe irrationally, in terms of what you could have done." She talks about how, when writing about her uncle's fateful decision to declare at Customs that he was seeking asylum instead of simply presenting his travel visa, she'd had the desperate desire to jump into the narrative and say, "No, don't do it!" She recalls many similar moments that made the writing especially difficult. "There were all these things where I wish I'd done this, I wish I'd done that. There's an irrational desire to try to save them again, even though I know I did everything I could. You want a different ending. And that was the hardest part. If it were fiction, I could change it—I could change the outcome."

Danticat articulates a feeling expressed by many of the writers I've spoken with who have written specifically about loss. "You read these memoirs, especially grief memoirs, and there's always a moment that the person writing the memoir wants to take back.

Wants to rewrite. Wants to change." I know that moment. I've encountered it in my own writing.

For Danticat, what she calls "the blissful distraction of having a newborn" helped her to cope with these hardest of moments in her writing process. "I don't know how I would have written it if I was alone in a house, you know? Just alone in a room with the material. But I had a little baby. I had to move forward."

Despite the pain in the process, Danticat says there was also a measure of comfort. "I felt like the worst had already happened, so the writing itself was very helpful. I didn't want this material to haunt me forever. I found the writing process itself very healing." She continues, "One thing that really helped was that at some point I said to myself, 'Why am I writing this?' And then I wrote that part that we talked about in the beginning [the words from her opening chapter: "I am writing this only because they can't."]. Once I knew why I was writing it, then the story was much easier to tell."

About halfway through working on the book, Danticat started to understand what parts of the story needed to be told and what parts she could leave out. "After a while, in the process, you have some distance, and you start thinking of it as *a* story, not as *your* story. That's a helpful distance, because that's when you get it out of being like your diary." She explains that this is an important message she shares with young people who want to write memoir. "It seems like everybody writes memoir because we can write a very heartfelt thing on Facebook and get a lot of people to respond. It really becomes memoir, though, when you open up space for others to enter—when it becomes about more than you, or your family, or your own personal feelings."

"Did you talk about any of it with your family while you were writing the book?" I ask. Danticat has three younger brothers, and her mother was still living at the time.

Danticat says she doesn't talk to many people about her writing in progress. "I feel very vulnerable in the period where it's happening. If they criticize, it might lead you to kill something because you are giving more value to their opinion than perhaps even they are. I've been thrown off by something people say in passing that they don't even remember saying later on, so I keep things to myself during the writing process itself, until I'm all done." She feels there's something unique to memoir in that vulnerability. "I think if I were teaching, I would definitely talk about the emotional element, like you're saying. I think for a lot of people, the first time they're addressing this material is when they're writing it. It's really hard to do without sentimentality. There's also an element of the ways that people respond to memoir that feels very personal. They're not just talking about your work; they're talking about your life."

Danticat didn't show the book to her brothers until it was finished. "My mother did ask me not to put her in the book. I felt like she wanted that to be respected. It was the men's stories, so it wasn't too difficult to leave her mostly out." She grins. "I did say to her, 'Well, you're in it a little.'"

Danticat had written and published seven books before *Brother, I'm Dying* came out in 2007. But the experience of completing this book was dramatically different for her. "I rarely remember when I finish books, because my books never really feel done to me until they're printed. But this day I remember so clearly. I remember where I was. I was at my little desk in a room that was also at the time the baby's room [she and Boyer had been renovating their house in stages, moving room to room], and I remember that day when I wrote the last word. Like, I can see it. And I knew it was done."

"What did that feel like for you?"

"There was really a sense of relief in that." In the pause that follows, I see a flicker of something else in her eyes. Quietly, she adds, "There was also a deep sense of sadness." She doesn't need to elaborate. I intimately understand the finality of closing the story of someone you love.

Though she hadn't shared it with them in process, Danticat's brothers were the first people she sent the finished draft to, and she did tell them that if they wanted her to take anything out, she would. "I felt like it was a thing—especially with my father—that we all experienced together, so I wanted their input." She gives me a sly smile and adds, "Sometimes you ask questions you know the answers to, and I already knew that they wouldn't be forcefully against it."

She laughs about the fact that one of her brothers did ask, "as brothers are wont to," why the book was all about her. "I answered, 'Because I'm writing it.'" This view from others who have shared in the experience that the writing is slanted seems common. Danticat also experienced something rare. Her tone softens when she says, "My youngest brother was just sweet about it. He said, 'Wow. It's just like I remember it.' And that's exactly what we want the subjects of memoir to say."

The year before the publication of *Brother, I'm Dying*, the ethics of writing memoir and truth telling were called into question with the very public revelations that James Frey, author of *A Million Little Pieces*, fabricated crucial episodes in his story. Similar to Monica Wood, who worried about people questioning the subjectivity of her memory, Danticat says that this climate of distrust made her hypervigilant about fact checking the details in her book, particularly the details surrounding her uncle's death. "That's where the documents were important," she explains. "And I'm glad I wrote it with such good proximity to the events, because things were still raw, the emotions were still raw. I felt really comfortable that I'd said everything that I wanted to say."

And though there were a few bizarre responses, like the reviewer who obsessed over why she hadn't talked anywhere in the book about the novel she had coming out that year, she says, "Overall the response was really beautiful. People will say, 'This is my story,' and they're not always the people you are expecting. They're not always the immigrants. They may be people who will say, 'My father died,' or people who grew up away from their family. It's really interesting to see what threads people pull out of a memoir. Sometimes it's not what the writer had intended at all, but there's something about it that speaks to them."

Danticat says she jokes all the time that she'd intended for her core audience to be TSA agents or immigration officers—"People like that who see the mass of humanity before them—to remind them that those people are individuals too." Though the initial TSA response to the press around Danticat's story became increasingly nasty, the reality is that Danticat's memoir has given a deeply personal face to so many others who've endured or are enduring similar injustices to those experienced by her Uncle Joseph. "I think part of the fire of the memoir was that I didn't want this to happen to another family. I realized, the more I talked about it and the more I met other families, how common this was and how little people knew about it. It's too late for us, but I don't want this to happen to other people."

Danticat tilts her head, and one of her silver chandelier earrings brushes her shoulder. Her expression is thoughtful when she articulates another aspiration she had in writing her memoir. "I think I realized at some point in the editing process that I wanted the book to be art. That I wanted it to be something people could read years from now too."

In 1994, after Danticat's first novel, *Breath, Eyes, Memory*, was published, the *New York Times Magazine* named her one of thirty writers and artists under thirty poised to transform American culture over the next thirty years. There's no doubt Danticat is living into that forecast. Her work has opened the door for necessary dialogue about immigration reform and the urgent need to change policy. After writing *Brother, I'm Dying*, she was invited to provide personal testimony at a congressional hearing. Since then, she's written influential essays, given powerful interviews, and shared her family's story again and again. The book is a required text for many first-year college seminars across the country. Last year, the National Endowment for the Arts chose *Brother, I'm Dying* as one of its "Big Reads," the first nonfiction book to receive the prestigious honor.

Yet, despite its widespread public influence, Danticat has not lost ownership of the personal story enveloped in her memoir's pages. "This is a sliver of the story. If I told every single thing, it would be like *War and Peace*, so there's still plenty left over for me. There are plenty of private moments that are mine." I remember Mark Doty's relief at making this same discovery, that there were still memories that belonged only to him, despite what he'd shared with the public in *Heaven's Coast*.

I can't help expressing my own relief at hearing Danticat say these words. My fears that I'll somehow lose my connection to strands of my story by bringing it into the larger sphere of the AIDS crisis often creep in.

"In terms of your process, it's important to know that it's doable," she tells me, her contagious optimism flowing through her words. "It's survivable. It's actually even helpful, because once you have the story wrapped up somewhere, you can dip in anytime. It's like a treasure chest with little pieces you can go in and look at, and step out."

Listening to Danticat speak in these final moments of our conversation is like moving into an embrace. Her quiet conviction gives me confidence. She rests her hand on the cover of her memoir. "I feel like this is the most beautiful memorial I could have created for my uncle and father. They're extraordinary to me, but their lives might not have meant anything to a lot of people. This was a way to honor them. Even as it's published and it's out there and time goes away, it becomes another kind of grief site. A place I can always go."

CHAPTER 12

Marianne Leone

· Jesse: A Mother's Story

I'm nervous as I drive up the long driveway to the modest, shingled house that backs onto a reed-filled tidal marsh in this small, maritime town on Massachusetts' South Shore. "Be cool, Melanie," I repeat out loud for maybe the thousandth time since I left my own house two hours earlier. I try to convince myself that this is no different than meeting anyone for the first time. Just be yourself, I think. Let them be themselves. And whatever you do, do not make an ass of yourself by behaving like a star-struck imbecile.

But as I walk the path to the front door, I can't help letting a tinge of excitement leak into my resolve. Because here's the thing: this meeting *is* a little bit different. Apart from her notoriety as an author, Marianne Leone is an established television and film star and screenwriter. Her husband, Chris Cooper, is an Academy Award–winning actor. And she's invited me to their home for lunch.

However, it's not their acting careers I'm interested in today. Let me qualify that: I'm *interested*, but their successes on the big screen have nothing to do with my visit. I'm here to talk about

Jesse. Jesse, their beautiful son whose life and death and legacy compelled Leone to write the memoir *Jesse: A Mother's Story*. A memoir that broke my heart and filled it at the same time.

Clutching the bouquet of flowers I've brought, I ring the bell. A chorus of barks begins, and I hear commands to "Settle" and "Be good, you two" before the door opens to a small woman, her blond hair cut to her chin, her vibrant, welcoming smile enhanced by red-painted lips. At her feet, two white-curled dogs I assume are some sort of poodle mix, shuffle and strut, discharging warning barks as she steers me in and leads me from the landing up the steps that divide the split-level, raised ranch. "They'll cut it out in a minute when they realize you aren't a threat," Leone says, thanking me for the flowers and setting them down on the kitchen counter. She offers to make me a cup of tea and urges me to take a seat at the table.

The kitchen, family room, and dining area are all part of one spacious room that opens to a back deck overlooking the marsh. The space is homey and inviting, collections of knickknacks and framed photographs adorning walls and shelves, and it's characterized by the general disorder of daily living—stacks of papers, books, and letters on the buffet next to the table, pots and dishes on the counters. I do note the unmistakable golden statuette that stands amidst the clutter on the buffet, but the Oscar is not the piece in the room that draws the eye.

Instead, my gaze settles on a tall easel against the far wall, a large canvas painting resting on its edge. The portrait is obviously Jesse, dark-eyed and full-lipped, feathered wings springing from his back, rays of light streaming down from above. "We had that commissioned when Jesse was four," Leone explains as she sets a steaming cup of tea in front of me. "It wasn't a death thing," she adds. "We're not that creepy." Her sardonic candor reinforces what I already know from reading her book: Marianne Leone has a great sense of humor.

Since my arrival, the dogs, Lucky and Frenchy, have decided I'm not there to hurt anybody and settle down on an oversized stuffed chair next to the table. "I love the hardwood," I say, commenting on the weathered flooring.

"It needs to be refinished," she answers.

I think about my own hardwood scratched all over by Wally, our two-year-old yellow Lab, and say something about how dogs can give floors a beating over time.

"Most of the marks are from Jess's wheelchair," she replies, her tone matter-of-fact.

I distinguish a well-worn path on the floorboards from the hallway to the table. Of course, I think, a stab of sadness tightening my chest. For a moment, I'm at a loss for words.

Leone is not the sort of person who needs an invitation to speak, though, so the silence doesn't last. I warm right away to her frank, no-holds-barred style of conversation.

"You should know this about me," she begins with a deep laugh, steering my focus in a lighter direction. "I have real problems with impulse control. I don't have good impulse control. I never have."

I'm delighted by this revelation because it means I'm assured of getting exactly what I'm looking for: an honest, unfiltered conversation about how she managed to write her book. How she managed to journey through the grief of her son's death to tell the story of his beautiful life.

In 1987, Jesse was born two and a half months early and developed cerebral palsy after suffering a cerebral hemorrhage. He was a quadriplegic, nonverbal, and contended with daily seizures. He was also handsome, funny, incredibly smart, creative, and deeply sensitive. Leone and Cooper fought an uphill battle to get educators to see these qualities beyond Jesse's disability. But Leone's unwavering resolve, her deliberate decision to become "a mother from hell," as she refers to herself in the memoir, and devote her life to advocating for her son, as well as the many lessons he taught her in the process, are the pulse of this story. In January of 2005, Jesse died suddenly. Leone and Cooper discovered him unresponsive in his bed on that terrible morning. He was seventeen years old.

Though Leone's story has connected her with hundreds of parents involved in the same struggle, and it has given her agency as an advocate for children with disabilities, she admits that she didn't write the book with the intention of helping other parents. "I didn't really give a shit at the time. Frankly, it was selfishly so I could spend lots of time with Jesse," she says. "It was totally about being with him." ·

Three months after Jesse died, Leone wrote an essay that appeared in the *Boston Globe* called "He Was Our Touchstone." She explains, "I really believe that first essay did come out of pain, but I felt like, I just have to give voice to him. I just have to re-create him. I have to talk about his life and the impact."

But then, Leone got sick. Cancer. A tumor in her gut that ironically weighed what Jesse had weighed at birth. What she began to call the "Not-Jesse." She tells me now, "I was dying for a while. My body was so outta here, and all of my focus was on that." When surgeons at Massachusetts General Hospital removed the tumor, they discovered the cancer had not spread. Leone knew she was going to live, and that's when she responded to the pull to write this book about her son.

"Part of it too is honoring the worth of that person's life, especially so in a kid like Jesse, where there were people who were taking away the worth of his life, always, always taking it away," she explains. "There's a part of you as his mother that wants to say his life was *really* worth something. So, there was that."

"Did you ever worry that you wouldn't be able to do him justice through your writing?"

"Yes, yes," Leone nods. "I had fear of that. I did have fear of not bringing him to life."

"How did you work through that fear?" I tell her I'm asking because trying to re-create a life as large as my dad's, and containing it within words on the page, has been an ongoing stumbling block.

"I think you've just got to work through that. Get out of your own head. It's self-consciousness, and self-consciousness is a destroyer of creativity." She pauses, and then adds, "You know what? Put your attention totally on him. Think of it as between you and him, and don't think about who else is going to be reading it. Think about it as between the two of you."

For Leone, the mindset that she was in partnership with Jesse gave her comfort during what felt like a seriously intimidating process. Although she'd written screenplays for years, the idea of writing this book was really frightening. "I had major fear of prose because I honored it far more than I did writing screenplay. This is the category of Joyce and Colette," she says, laughing.

To conquer the fear hurdle, she decided to join Grub Street, a Boston-based community of writers helping writers that offers classes, workshops, and conferences for both emerging and established writers. She enrolled in a memoir class. "Joining Grub Street did ameliorate the terror somewhat because I was in the company of other people." There, she found the prompting she needed to tell more of her experience. "Now I'm in a group of people who are really egging me on, who are giving me really positive feedback. And then your ego gets involved too, and it's like, I have to finish this now. Too many people know I've started it."

I get it. Without my own MFA program and its deadlines and workshops and mentors, I know I couldn't have even begun the journey of writing my own hard story. I needed other people too. People, like Marianne Leone, who understand exactly what it's like to tug threads of experience out of the darkness and find some glimmers of light.

Revisiting the memories of Jesse's life allowed her to do just that. "Despite the pain that it called up, especially writing about the painful parts—the seizures, the fighting with the school, the injustices that were dealt him, all of that." She stops before saying, "Maybe I've hazily reconstructed it the way you do with birth, but for me, the majority of the time spent was with good memories too, you know? I just recently used the scene again in a speech I gave, the scene of sitting with him on the couch and him finding the first letter of his name and me being determined that he would learn and go to school. It's great to call up that kind of memory. So that sustained me, that sustained me emotionally through some of the really hard parts of doing it."

She can readily identify the parts that were most difficult to write. "The seizures. The seizure chapter was the hardest." She exhales like she's pushing back at the pain of those memories. "That was the hardest to deal with, and that's what killed him. And in fact," she says, "of course like anybody trying to avoid pain, I left it toward the end."

"Did you ever think of leaving those parts out?"

"No," she responds. "I really was determined to be truthful. I put in all my fears, I hope."

And when writing about those fears felt dark for her, she says, pointing through the window to the marsh behind the house, "the phragmites were very helpful." In her book, Leone writes about hacking at the reeds in that marsh as a vehicle for her pain and frustration when she struggled with the writing and especially when she couldn't conjure the images of Jesse that she wanted. "Time recedes and there is only the curtain of reeds before me, impenetrable, like a veil. [. . .] I need to break through to the green water that moves in and out of its muddy bed twice a day, as if the Jones River will somehow become the River Styx that carries me to Jesse."

Leone also found solace in other people's hard stories. Abigail Thomas's *A Three Dog Life* (which Leone references in her memoir) was a particular influence for her. "And that actually gave me the courage to realize that I didn't have to abandon my sense of humor while I was writing about a subject that was ostentatiously tragic. And the other great thing was realizing that I didn't have to follow some sort of beginning-middle-and-end thing with the book."

Leone's sometimes irreverent sense of humor is a distinctive characteristic of her memoir. "I credit the irreverence to my mother, the ultimate irreverent role model," she says, laughing when I mention it. I ask Leone if she meant to give readers some comic relief when she was writing the book. "I don't know that I consciously used humor. I think it was always a part of our lives, with Jesse and in our marriage, and that is why it was present in the memoir. Also, there was a lot of laughter and humor involving our son—he always was the first person at the table to get the joke, and I think unconsciously, I brought that to the memoir as a tribute to his memory."

"Were there moments when you wondered if you *should* be writing about some of the things in your story?" I ask, voicing the tension that plagues me in my own process.

"Yes," Leone begins, but then self-corrects. "Although, I didn't as I was doing it. That's what is so frightening." She smiles and reiterates her impulse-control problems. "It amazes me now that Chris didn't read this until it was done. So that's kind of amazing, that I'm exposing him like this. But that's my trust in him too."

She continues, "I didn't even think about the long-term effects until after I'd finished. Which is scary," she adds. "I'll give you an example. When the lawyers were vetting it, the lawyer calls me and he says, 'So you live in a small town, right?' And I go, 'Yeah.' He says, 'So, the aide that you describe is still there. You might want to think about making her physical attributes different.'"

"Did you?" I ask, feeling the same grip of anger I'd felt when I'd read the scene in Leone's book about this woman who'd callously dismissed Jesse as an actual person in front of his caregiver with words like "he don't belong here" and "we both know where he's gonna end up."

"Well, immediately after he said that I pictured her marauding me at the mall or something," she chuckles. Then, her voice quiets. "But, I didn't."

I admired Leone's tenacity when I read her story for the first time. I admire it even more now. She doesn't need to say what we both know to be true, what Richard Hoffman so clearly demonstrated when he wrote *Half the House* and named his abuser.

The people in these stories who've done the most damage haven't earned the right to be completely anonymous. Leone does add, "I'm working on forgiveness. I always say, 'I'm *working* on forgiveness.'"

Though skeptical of what she calls "metaphysical or spiritual stuff," Leone holds fast to the belief that Jesse was with her through the process of writing this book and continues to remain close. "I feel like I had his help. Jesse was a great teacher. I tapped into my teacher. If the prose is poetic, it's because that was our communication, and we're communicating through this."

She tells me about the day she received the edited manuscript and how she sat out on the back deck where she and Jesse used to sit together on the glider and looked through the copy. While she was looking, a big, beautiful dragonfly lighted on the pages. She leans closer, passion weaving its way into her words, and I feel the prickle of goose bumps on my skin as I sense where this story is headed. "I say, 'Jesse, I hope you like your book.' And then I say, 'If it's you, come and sit on my hand.' And then it does." She sits back and stretches her arms wide. "It was another one of those moments where the universe cracks open a little bit."

We break for lunch, and it's then that I meet her husband. Chris Cooper emerges from the lower level of the house where he's been cleaning for a houseguest arriving the next day. When Leone tells me the name of the well-known actress who'll be staying overnight, I try to be nonchalant, but I'm not sure I pull it off.

Cooper is quiet and thoughtful, almost shy, a solid foil to his wife's spirited personality. As we talk off the record over a delicious prosciutto and vegetable soup, I observe a beautiful chemistry between them. Cooper's support of his wife and her endeavors is obvious from the way he listens intently, a hint of a smile playing on his lips. And her love and pride permeates everything she says about him and about his work. They've survived the unimaginable together, and as they talk to me about Jesse, I watch them travel together to what Leone describes in her book as "a place where words are no longer needed to evoke the profound memories of the events that shaped us."

After lunch, Cooper and Leone give me a full tour of the house. We begin downstairs. "It's a lot different now," Leone tells me of the renovated space, and I don't miss the wistful note in her voice. There's a section in her book where she describes the beginnings of this home remodeling project: "We're not moving, but we're moving on. Everything will change. But I hate change, and I hate Chris for instigating this one." Now, though, her praise of Cooper's skilled craftsmanship and the way she runs her hand along the fine detailing of the woodwork tell me that any resentment she might have had has long since disappeared. They show me the guest room that once belonged to Brandy, Jesse's former caretaker. They walk me past the new exercise pool that replaced Jesse's indoor therapy pool. They note where Jesse's elevator used to be. Their son's missing presence can be felt in each noted change.

After the downstairs tour, Cooper returns to his work, and Leone and I head back upstairs to resume our discussion. When we reach the top of the landing, she invites me to look inside Jesse's room. Lord of the Rings posters adorn the walls, and a bookshelf displays photos and memorabilia typical of a teenage boy. "This isn't Jesse's," Leone says, resting her hand on the dark wood headboard of the double bed in the center of the room. "His bed is in our old room." We do not linger. I understand that this is sacred space.

Before we sit again at the table, Leone brings out two thick folders for me to inspect. They contain many of the notes she's received since publishing her book in 2011. I sift through the stacks of handwritten cards and letters, e-mails, snapshots of children of varying ages. These letters come from parents with disabled children, parents who have lost a child, public school teachers, specialists. They all carry the same message in slightly different words: *Thank you.*

"Some of these made me cry outright," Leone says as I leaf through the messages of appreciation. "Some of these people, realizing what they deal with, was heartbreaking to me. I didn't think it would be this outpouring. I didn't know what to expect. You ease other people's pain and it bounces back on you."

Less than a year from now, a dear friend of mine will lose her ten-year-old son, also a quadriplegic with CP, in the identical way Jesse died, suffering a seizure sometime in the night. I will give her Leone's book to read if and when she feels ready. A few days before the first anniversary of her son's death, my friend will send me a note expressing how familiar and comforting Leone's story is for her. When I e-mail Leone to tell her that Jesse's story is continuing to touch lives, she writes back, "It makes me happy to think that the book will give her some measure of comfort. Mourning is so hard."

Among the responses Leone has received, some of the most meaningful have come from teachers—the audience she'd really wanted to hear Jesse's story and her perspective as a parent who'd advocated for her child's basic right to a free and appropriate public education in the least restrictive environment. "There was one teacher, even before the book was finished, who wrote to me and said, 'I use your essay as a teaching mechanism in my eighth-grade class.' And she sent me essays that the kids wrote about it." To her delight, Leone's memoir is being used in the teacher education programs at Boston University and Bridgewater State University.

Leone's honesty attracts people to her story. "A lot of people tell me they read my book in one sitting. Like, they devour it." She grows thoughtful. "I think it's because they're looking for—I was the same way—I was looking for a like situation. I wanted to hear from someone else who was dealing the same way I was."

I realize this is exactly why I love Leone's book and devoured it, too. Her way of dealing feels refreshingly real. I'm curious whether she's had any regrets about making her story public, despite the positive response. "Do you feel like you gave anything up?"

She tells me there have been moments. Moments when she's regretted sharing Jesse. Moments when she's wished she'd kept him all to herself. "Grief is like a horrible sniper that comes out of nowhere, and you have these moments where you just unexpectedly fall into a three-day vortex. And in the vortex you feel like: You can't have him. He's mine. I will warn you, that happens. It's like *The Giver*," she says, referencing the young-adult book by Lois Lowry. "By letting go the memory, it's gone." But she reassures me that it's never been a permanent feeling. "What balances that, though, is the people who say, 'I feel like I know Jesse. I feel like I know him now.' That makes me really happy because his life ended too soon."

Leone is genuinely happy that she was able to write this book. She's happy to have honored her son. To have honored his worth. But she doesn't mince words as we wrap up our conversation. "I think what you're hoping I'm going to tell you is that I had this great pain and that writing this book took the great pain away. And I will tell you that with grief, I mean, there is a lessening of the immediacy." She repeats those words, "There is a lessening of the immediacy. I wish I could say the pain goes away, but I do not think that there's a lessening of pain. It's just different."

I gaze again at the portrait of angel-winged Jesse on the easel. I retrace the house tour Cooper and Leone gave me after we'd finished eating, and I picture the shelves in Jesse's bedroom that still hold his favorite books, small toys, a worn teddy bear. I think of the tears I glimpsed in Cooper's eyes before he turned toward the window when Leone shared some of their family stories over lunch. I glance at the track marks from Jesse's wheelchair on the floor that "needs to be refinished," but has not been.

I look at Leone sitting across from me, the light in her eyes a beacon of courage. The pain is still here, but so are you, Marianne. And that reality fills me with hope.

CHAPTER 13

Jerald Walker

· *Street Shadow: A Memoir of Race,
Rebellion, and Redemption*
· *The World in Flames: A Black Boyhood
in a White Supremacist Doomsday Cult*

Emerson College, easily overlooked if you don't know it's there,
is nestled in the heart of Boston's Theater District, at the intersection of Boylston and Tremont Streets. It borders the south-
east end of the Boston Common, the oldest public park in the
United States. Emerson's Ansin Building, a fourteen-story, art
deco structure, houses many of the college's academic and ad-
ministrative departments, including the Department of Writing,
Literature, and Publishing.

On a late Wednesday afternoon at the end of January, I join a
stream of students entering the building and crowd onto an elevator to travel to the twelfth floor. As I begin checking out numbers
on office doors in search of #1214, a goateed, African American
man in his early fifties approaches with hand outstretched. I recognize him as Jerald Walker from the photo I'd seen of him on
the department's faculty page (minus the goatee).

"Melanie?" he asks, giving me a questioning smile.

142

"Yes," I say, reaching for his hand and warming to him right away. His calm demeanor relaxes any nerves I might be feeling. Walker guides me around a center bay of cubicles to his office. Stepping inside, I take in the beautiful space: a corner room with two intersecting walls of windows that showcase a breathtaking view of the city. Two leather armchairs angle toward a low round table. I choose the one with the view. Walker's desk sits against an interior wall, and stacks of papers and folders and books—staples of any writing professor's clutter—garnish its surface. An open-backed bookcase hangs above the desk, its shelves lined with titles; one catches my eye: Richard Hoffman's *Love & Fury*. Hoffman is a faculty colleague of Walker's here at Emerson.

The path to literary success that brought Walker to this stunning office and his current position as associate professor at Emerson is the context for my visit. And Walker's journey to overcome the adversity of his upbringing to realize this success is the basis for his celebrated first memoir, *Street Shadows*, winner of the 2011 PEN New England/L. L. Winship Award for Nonfiction and *Kirkus Reviews*' 2010 Best Memoir of the Year.

Walker's second memoir, *The World in Flames: A Black Boyhood in a White Supremacist Doomsday Cult*—"That should do it!" Walker laughs when he reveals the dramatic new subtitle—is a prequel to the first. When I meet with Walker, the book is still in production with Beacon Press. Knowing I was meeting with Walker, my editor gave me an advance copy to read.

"You are maybe one of the very few people to have read both books then," Walker reflects when I tell him. "Only my wife and maybe four other people have read *Street Shadows* and this one."

The privilege in having read both memoirs is that I've gained a much rounder picture of Walker's life and story than those who've only read *Street Shadows*. In so many visible ways, the second memoir—the story of Walker's family's deep involvement with Herbert Armstrong's Worldwide Church of God, an end-of-the-world prophesying, totalitarian organization, and its impact on Walker's childhood—informs the first. Walker wishes that more of the material from the second book had appeared in his original memoir. "The slice of life that *Street Shadows* contains is a very small part of my youth and does not tell the full picture," Walker laments. "I kind of wish the two books could be sold together. A boxed set."

Walker is also pragmatic enough to know that the success of the first memoir was a likely catalyst for the publication of the second. "I also wanted my story to be told, and if that was the section I could start with, then so be it. I would tell this section of it."

Street Shadows begins at a moment of crisis for Walker, when his friend Greg is shot and killed at the apartment where he'd recently started selling dope, just an hour after Walker left there with two grams of coke in his pocket. This moment frames the story, told in alternating sequences of time, of Walker's redemptive struggle toward a life he could be proud of, out from the "urban undertow" of the Chicago neighborhood streets that had pulled him down when he was fourteen years old. The tale, harrowing and heartbreaking at times, warm and hopeful at others, is masterfully written by a man whose honest examination of his own choices, and profound empathy towards the choices of others, carries readers beyond what might be considered the stereotypical inner-city experience of drugs and gangs, to a very personal history shaped by incredible circumstances.

Walker, like so many other writers who trained first in fiction, is a reluctant memoirist. "I did not want to be on the record as the author of my own life," he tells me when he begins explaining the difficult decision to start telling this story. He studied at the University of Iowa, pursuing an MFA in fiction. "I was telling these autobiographical stories that were inner-city, with some race, but [also] drugs and alcohol, and the stuff that I knew, but I didn't want to be the protagonist of the stories. I deliberately sort of disguised myself in my stories." He laughs. "Not very well, though. Instead of Jerald Walker, I'd be Walk Jerald or something."

Among the 99 percent white population at Iowa who came from a background that in no way resembled Walker's, he wanted to avoid being the stereotypical black guy with the stereotypical stories about his life. "I was simply there as the reporter of that life. But it wasn't me. Not my life at all. I just heard these things." He adds, "I was so ashamed of the many things I had done and gone through."

So, for the three years he studied at Iowa, Walker hid behind this veil. And afterwards, when he continued to write fiction, mainly short stories, he found very limited success. He grins and qualifies, "Which is to say I couldn't publish anything. Nothing was working."

Walker's wife, Brenda Molife—a former art history professor, now vice president of the Bridgewater State University Foundation—gave him the shove he needed to break free from his preset expectations for his writing. "Maybe ten years ago, she told me, 'You know what? This fiction thing is kind of not working out yet. Why don't you write nonfiction? Why don't you write an essay about your experiences instead of a short story?'"

Straightening his back and puffing out his chest with false machismo, Walker says, "I told her she was nuts. I'm a fiction writer. And I proceeded to list all the great short story writers I'd soon be in company with." Molife didn't back down. She urged him to try writing an essay. Just once.

"So I wrote an essay about my experience in a writing workshop with James Alan McPherson when I had a difficult time in his class." A version of the essay appears in *Street Shadows*. In an ironic twist, McPherson called Walker out in the workshop as a fraud because Walker's material dealt with subject matter McPherson didn't feel Walker had the authority to write about. "He'd bought into my myth of me not being from that background. My whole plan of disguising myself backfired in a way, because he believed me to be an inauthentic narrator of those experiences."

Walker wrote the essay in two days. He felt he'd done his duty and appeased his wife. "She asked, 'Well what are you going to do with it?'" Walker sent it to the *Iowa Review*, and six days later, they accepted it for publication. Four months after that, Robert Atwan, series editor of *The Best American Essays*, recommended Walker's essay to guest editor David Foster Wallace, who selected it for the 2007 edition. He laughs. "And my wife said, 'Told you.'"

Walker wrote more essays, some of which he recycled from fictional pieces he'd written at Iowa. And each one he wrote got published. "It was like magic," he says. And the more he wrote, the more he understood why these stories hadn't worked as fiction. "While I was still trying to hide behind fiction, the stories just weren't clicking. Once I fully accepted that I would have to expose myself, the stories came alive."

The exposure wasn't easy for Walker, though. "As I mentioned, I felt a tremendous amount of guilt for some of my behavior and a lot of embarrassment, because the teenager that I was, was not the teenager that my parents groomed me to be. I had betrayed their teaching and their discipline and their values. I didn't really want to write these things."

Walker credits his wife with helping him past that hurdle, too. "She said, 'But look at how the story ends. Everything has turned out well for you. You turned your whole life around. While you went off track and went into some pretty dark places, it was your parents' teachings that brought you back.'"

With that focus on the redemptive part of his story, Walker was able to face his shame and guilt honestly. "It freed me up. I was at peace with what I saw on the page when I wrote nonfiction. In a way it allowed me to confess my sins and to own them. It was like going through the mistakes in my life one by one and trying to find some redemptive quality in each one. Like a prisoner in a cell, I was marking the lines on the wall." He holds up an imaginary piece of chalk and mimes making checkmarks in the air. "Okay, that one's done, and that one's done, and that one's done. I would go through these different episodes of my life and address them in a way that I could come to terms with the experience. And each time I did that successfully, I felt myself becoming more proud of who I am and more accepting of who I am."

Walker's accumulated essays were the springboards to *Street Shadows*. An agent saw one essay in the *Chronicle of Higher Education* and asked if he had more. Walker sent him about twenty published essays and said he hoped to write a collection. The agent discouraged him from that approach, saying that no one would buy a collection of essays from an unknown. He told him it needed to have a narrative arc. It needed to be a memoir. Walker puffs out his chest again and cracks a rueful smile. "I said, 'I'm not a memoirist. I'm an essayist.' And the agent said, 'Do you want to sell a book?' I said, 'Yes.' He asked, 'Then are you a memoirist?' I said, 'Yes. Yes I am.'"

What helped Walker in this transition is that he still approached the memoir as a collection. Of the stories he wanted to include, 75 percent were already written as essays, so it was a matter of writing the essays that filled in the gaps. He had to find the bridges between them. "That helped me as a first-time memoirist, to have that structure sort of outlined for me."

Walker says, too, like many of the reluctant memoirists in this book, that he likely would never have been able to write one of those essays had he not trained first as a fiction writer. "I think it saved me," he admits. "The craft of storytelling is at the heart of what I do as an essayist. I know the importance of stories, and I know the importance of character, and I know the importance of plotting, of conflict."

The act of writing those essays to begin with and to complete the ones that filled in the gaps was, nonetheless, a painful process. "I cried a lot writing this book," he says. "But a lot of it was like an out-of-body experience. At some point I stopped seeing the 'I' as me, and I started seeing the 'I' as a character I was writing about. Often, I would feel so bad for the character Jerry in the book as a kid. As I saw myself writing my own story, and I knew I was going to make a bad decision, I couldn't alter it. I felt so bad for the choices I'd made, just seeing them on the page. Many times I brought myself to tears, but I was crying for the character on the page, more than I was crying for me as a person."

Walker's voice quiets as he reflects further. "I don't know if that's because it was so long ago, and I'm in such a different place now, but I hurt for the kid on the page. I felt like a father to that kid. I have two sons, and I would always imagine them making the choices that I made, and it would just break my heart all over again."

It was really through writing about them that Walker could see how those decisions had shaped so many of the shadows in his past. "When I was living through it, I was simply in the middle of this hurricane of activity and bad choices and bad decisions and bad outcomes, and I didn't reflect on it a whole lot at all. But when you write about it twenty years later and you really think about what you were going through and why you made certain decisions, it's heartbreaking."

Walker continues, "I wonder—and this is occurring to me just now—whether that's why I wanted to fictionalize the stories, so I could make different decisions for the character. And maybe that's why those fiction stories went astray. They were autobiographical, but my fictional characters always seemed to make slightly better choices. But the stories didn't work, so maybe it's the bad decisions that make good literature." In reflecting on how riveted I was by Walker's memoir, I have to surmise that in some ways, they do.

When Walker knew he was writing a book, a new fear took hold. "I knew I'd have a bigger audience, and then I knew that I would really have to have close family members and friends know about the stories that otherwise they never would have known about. And the hardest part for me was knowing that my mother was going to read these stories."

In light of this comment, it's surprising for me to hear that, apart from his wife, the one person with whom he did share his writing in process was his mother (his father had already died). A fascinating element to Walker's background is that he grew up in a home where both of his parents were blind. "As I finished writing a chapter, I would call her and read it. So I read the entire book to her so she could get the full story. And that's when she heard some stories that she would rather not have heard."

"How did you overcome the fear and risk you felt in bringing those closest to you into your intimate experiences?" I ask.

"It's my job as a writer, and especially as a nonfiction writer, to do things that I'm not entirely comfortable with. If I'm going to be true to this choice, then I have to tell the stories honestly." But it certainly wasn't easy for Walker. And many of the stories he had to tell were gut wrenching.

One of the most poignant for me is a scene in *Street Shadows* where he retells the events that ended in one of his closest childhood buddies being on death row after shooting and killing a mother of two boys, five and six, when the buddy hijacked her car. Walker imagines seeing him one last time and writes: "He was going to be executed and I was not, even though we were both assembly-line toys, manufactured with parts that weren't meant to last. Mine had—he'd hate me for that. But I'd hate him, too. Because for the entire visit, I'd be thinking about *my* two boys, aged four and six, and imagining them in a world, for no good reason, without a mother."

Walker tears up when I refer to that chapter, and he tells me it was one of the most difficult to write. "The hard moments usually snuck up on me. I didn't know I was writing that last sentence until I was writing it. The piece was supposed to be an essay about me lamenting Steve's life. I didn't realize it was about me lamenting what could happen to my kids because of someone like Steve until I typed that final sentence. I was bawling like crazy. I was blindsided like that. And for the other pieces in the book that are especially emotional, it happened like that. I found myself writing to a place that I didn't expect, and I'm not sure I could have gone to had I known what was there."

He laughs now. "I'm pretty sure that's better. If you are about to walk to the store at night and someone tells you, 'By the way, when you are a block away somebody is going to leap out of an alley,' you probably don't go. But if you're just going and it happens, then you find yourself in it." He pauses. "I often found people leaping out of alleys as I wrote the book. And then I realized, well that happened, and I'm going to have to include it."

Walker asserts that finishing *Street Shadows* was a remarkable thing. "The process of having this book come about healed me in a way. I saw that my life had amounted to something that I could be pretty proud of. I had taken these things from my life that I had been so ashamed of and crafted them into art. Something important. Something valuable."

I recall Richard Hoffman speaking almost these exact words about finishing *Half the House*. The universal truth that healing emerges from making something beautiful out of trauma is a fundamental binding to all of these conversations.

"I had for so many years felt that I had wasted ten years of my life," Walker reflects. "And for the first time, when the book was finished, I saw that those ten years were probably the most important ten years of my life, because they'd made me who I am and they'd also made me produce something that was ultimately valuable."

Walker has seen that value again and again when he's given readings to high school kids living in difficult communities, not unlike his own on the south side of Chicago. "To know that these stories in some way had students say, 'You know what? Maybe my life can turn out in a way that I can be proud of as a story.' That was incredibly important to me."

The responses that have been most meaningful to Walker, though, have come from people who had helped him throughout his life in times of great need. "I think Russell Baker mentioned about his memoir *Growing Up* that the reason why he wrote it was so that he could pay tribute to important people in his life. I got to do that in *Street Shadows* with all the people who at random moments came into my life and passed me along to the next good place. It was nice to hear people recognize that I didn't at any point position myself as some sort of superhero who by the sheer strength of my personality managed to pull myself out of these dire straits. I had help. I couldn't have done it without the people who I try to bring some attention to throughout the book."

Walker recounts one beautiful encounter after *Street Shadows* was published. Professor Homewood, the teacher in his memoir who encouraged him to pursue writing and paid for his education at the University of Iowa, has, in the years since, remained a close friend. Now in his eighties, Professor Homewood has been retired for quite some time. "When I was finishing the book, I called him and said, 'I'm going to send it to you soon. I'm giving a reading at the Chicago Public Library, and I'd love for you to be there.'" Homewood was full of praise, but he also told Walker some devastating news: he was suffering from macular degeneration and could barely see. Walker sent him the book anyway.

On the night of the reading, Walker arrived at the venue and reserved a seat for Professor Homewood amidst the crowd of former neighbors and friends. He waited in the lobby, hoping his former mentor would show up. The elevator doors opened up, and there was the professor, his arm balancing on a stranger's shoulder. "I said, 'Professor Homewood, it's me. Jerry.' And he put his hands on my shoulders, and he said, 'Jerry, my dear boy'—he always called me 'My dear boy'—'My dear boy, I did it. I managed to read your book. And how fitting it is that yours is the last one I'll ever read.'" Walker says they were both crying, but he had the opportunity to lead Professor Homewood to his reserved seat, and before the reading, Walker asked him to stand so he could tell the audience that the reading and the book were dedicated to this man, the teacher who had made it all possible.

I'm in tears at the end of Walker's telling, and so is he. "So that was fantastic," he finishes, his voice trembling. Responses like those had made the work feel significant.

A very different kind of response to *Street Shadows* was what led Walker to eventually write his second memoir, *The World in Flames*. "When people read *Street Shadows*, they don't know that the church experiences propelled us into that life on the streets. I don't think we would have gone that route with the recklessness that we did had we not been in the church and had the church not turned out to be what we thought it was."

Walker's publisher for *Street Shadows* urged him to downplay the religious aspect, though, wanting instead to market the book more as a sociological study of the inner-city, ghetto, black kid experience—even waiting to release it in February, Black History Month. "In some ways, the response has been kind of the opposite of what I was going for. That people contact me when there are questions of race that they would like to discuss has typecast me in some ways. They saw the book as a text on a certain condition, instead of a book that sought to make art out of an experience. I see myself as a writer who has some understanding of the art of storytelling, rather than being simply an expert on the inner-city black experience."

There was some peace, though, in knowing that he'd taken his experience in *Street Shadows* further than simply telling about his late teens and early adult years. "It went to me becoming an academic and becoming a parent, and at least told a part of my story that wasn't simply the stereotypical ghetto experience. But I always felt a nagging sensation that the motivation for that lifestyle was not included, and I think that was probably as important, if not more important, than the outcome of my life."

Writing *The World in Flames* satiated that feeling for Walker, because the memoir tells the fuller family story. "It was a completely different experience, but in some ways it was easier for me because I knew what the grand scheme was, and as it's the prequel to *Street Shadows*, I certainly knew where the ending was. I knew exactly where I was headed."

Perhaps that ease of writing accounts for some of the humor that shines from Walker's second memoir. When I ask him about that shift in tone, Walker replies, "If you think about it, it is a funny story—to be a black kid in a white supremacist doomsday cult. If that's not funny, then you're really going to have a sad story on your hands. The irony is simply embedded in story."

Walker goes on to talk about how humor can serve an important role in memoir. "I think in order to get this material to be something that people can accept in a way that's not overwhelmingly sad, you have to have these release points. When I saw an opportunity for them, which is to say when I remembered something that was funny that I thought would be important to the story, I made sure to include it. You have to have it, because there are some really sad parts too."

I know he's right because in reading the advance copy of the manuscript, I stretched the emotional gamut, laughing out loud in spots and openly crying in others.

Walker also cautions about the use of humor in memoir. "I don't say to my students, 'Don't forget, try to get at least four jokes per essay.'" He smiles. "I think it's just got to be part of who they are as writers and people, and that they'll find these opportunities for humor and levity."

Walker obviously can't speak to reader response for this second memoir since, as I speak with him, it's yet to be released, but he expounds on the feeling of finishing. "Before I wrote the book, I only saw the church and my parents' decision to join it as a way of making my life miserable. I carried that for so long. But the more I wrote the book, the more I could see that my parents simply wanted something good for me, and they made a bad choice. But it was for a good reason." By the time he was done, Walker had found a way to forgive his parents. "I stopped being so angry," he says. "By the end, I had saved my parents; I had pulled them from the precipice of being people who had made awful mistakes for which they could not be forgiven."

I understand that for Walker, both memoir-writing experiences have been about forgiveness and healing. In *Street Shadows* he wrote his way to forgiving himself for his bad choices. In *The World in Flames* he wrote toward a more generous vision of his imperfect parents and their choices for him. And in the process, he developed a deep appreciation for the closely examined life. "Until you start writing, you are blind to what you were living at the time. I went through life and made a lot of decisions that didn't make a lot of sense. I had to try to figure out in retrospect what my thought process was and try to piece together my psyche to understand that I was this poor lost boy making these decisions."

I begin to gather my things, preparing to leave Walker's office so he won't be late for his evening memoir class. He asks me a pointed question, "Do you ever worry that you'll run out of material?"

"I worry more that I'll always be writing about the *same* material," I reply.

"Would that be so bad?" he asks, and then adds. "I wonder sometimes about my material as a memoirist. Will I get tired of writing about my own experiences? And I think the answer is no. As long as there are people in my orbit who I think deserve some attention, I like being the vehicle to deliver it. My stories are kind of about me, but they're kind of not about me. They're about the people I encounter."

On my ride back down the elevator, I consider what Walker said. And I consider the people like Jerald Walker I've encountered in the writing of this book. If they're part of my material, then it's hard to see myself growing tired of it anytime soon.

CHAPTER 14

Kate Bornstein

· *A Queer and Pleasant Danger: The True Story of a Nice Jewish Boy Who Joins the Church of Scientology and Leaves Twelve Years Later to Become the Lovely Lady She Is Today*

The explanation of how I, in a black cocktail dress, my patent-leather pumps kicked off somewhere near a heap of clothes on the floor in the corner, end up reclining on a couple of pillows that rest against the wall at one end of Kate Bornstein's bed while she, dressed in loose leggings and an oversized sweater, lies across the other end, propped on an elbow, her stockinged feet hanging over the edge, is not actually as bizarre as the scene might initially sound.

I'd arrived in New York City by train the day before and planned to meet the performance artist, playwright, and author for dinner. Not uncharacteristically, my inexperience with New York's public transit and my miscalculation of the distance between my hotel in Brooklyn and Bornstein's home in Manhattan led to a hiccup in timing. We'd rescheduled our interview for this afternoon at the apartment she shares with longtime partner, performance artist, sex educator, and author Barbara Carrellas. The one glitch in the plan is that now that I realize the distance, I will have to go directly from meeting with Bornstein to a formal event for World AIDS Day, where I'll be reading. So, on this rainy December afternoon, I show up to their first-floor apartment in a three-story brownstone on a tree-lined street in East Harlem dressed a whole lot fancier than I normally would be for a casual afternoon of tea and conversation.

Carrellas greets me at the door and leads me up the stairs to the main living area, where I am also greeted by one of their two pugs, Piggle. She snuffles at my feet until I reach down and give her a scratch under her wrinkly, smushed face.

At first glance, it's not hard to tell that I've entered the home of creative literary artists who appear to collect their sources of inspiration. Piles of books are stacked on nearly every available surface, and an eclectic mix of miniature sculptures and knick-knacks, among them likenesses of the Buddha, congregate on the shelves. The walls display sketches of the human form and other framed prints in a range of styles and sizes.

Bornstein is sitting at the table finishing a bowl of soup, and as I hang my coat over the staircase railing, she turns in her seat, flashes me a charismatic smile, and declares, "Cancer free!" I welcome this news as way of introduction. Bornstein's health has been an ongoing concern since her diagnosis of chronic lymphocytic leukemia in 1996 and then lung cancer in 2012, nearly the same time the memoir I've come to discuss, *A Queer and Pleasant Danger*, was first published. After surgery and chemotherapy and radiation, she'd had a period of remission before a recurrence at the end of 2014. More aggressive treatments led to another period of remission, and the results of the follow-up scans she'd had earlier today are a confirmation that Bornstein remains in good health.

Bornstein brews me a cup of tea in her narrow galley kitchen, then ushers me into the living room to begin the interview. A shoji room divider stands next to a large aquarium—home to the pet turtle I'd read about in her bio, I assume, though I don't get a close look as I walk by. Just as we sit down and start our conversation, her housecleaner enters with a vacuum in tow. Turns out, we're in the one room of the apartment she's yet to clean. The noise of a vacuum and a recorded interview don't mix, so we decide to vacate. The only quiet option? Bornstein and Carrellas's bedroom, located down a short flight of stairs.

Which takes us back to the beginning and why Kate Bornstein and I spend the next hour and forty minutes of my visit lounging on her bed like two girls at a slumber party (except for the cocktail dress) sharing secrets. And when you think about the intimacies we're discussing about writing through our hardest of experiences, there's something just so fitting in ending up exactly here.

At one time, secrets defined Bornstein's life. She acted her way through her childhood and early adulthood, trying desperately to be someone she was not in order to live up to the pre-established expectations of being born Al Bornstein, first son of an accomplished New Jersey doctor. Now, sixty-seven years old, a self-titled "tranny" who chose sexual reassignment surgery in 1986, Bornstein is all about truth telling and being exactly who she is. "What I've tried to do with my theater and with this book as an extension of that is I've tried to break down the difference between who I am on stage and who I am in real life. I didn't want there to be any kind of posing or lying," she explains, her speech deliberate and thoughtful.

The rutted and complex trail that led to this magnetic, deeply compassionate woman with a brazen sense of humor stretched out across from me—decorated in tattoos and piercings, and with round, black-rimmed glasses, their lenses tinted pink, perched on her face—is neatly summed up in the lengthy subtitle of her book: "The true story of a nice Jewish boy who joins the Church of Scientology and leaves twelve years later to become the lovely lady she is today." But, as her gripping memoir reveals, becoming Kate Bornstein—queer icon and gender outlaw, considered one of today's foremost gender theorists, whose nuanced ideas of gender fluidity have opened space for many individuals who don't identify either as male or female—was anything but neat.

After twelve years of serving as an elite member of the Sea Organization, a religious order of the Church of Scientology, and working closely with Scientology founder, L. Ron Hubbard, Bornstein was accused of spying, excommunicated, and labeled a "suppressive person," an SP—what the church considers the epitome of true evil. Bornstein has been diagnosed with border-line personality disorder, suffered from deep bouts of depression, and contemplated suicide. She's lived with anorexia and PTSD. She is a sadomasochist who derives pleasure from pain and finds relief and gratification in cutting herself. And she hasn't been able to speak to or see her daughter, still a member of the Church of Scientology, for over thirty-five years. She's never met her two grandchildren.

"Not a day goes by that I don't think of her and want to be in touch with her," Bornstein says of her daughter. "But Scientology is a belief system where everything is black and white. There are no shades of gray. It's right or wrong. It's good or evil. And I'm evil."

Though the Church of Scientology has always had a strange and puzzling mystique to the outside world, it's not difficult to understand why Al Bornstein, a young man struggling with identity and seeking ways to end his life, would be drawn to a spiritual organization asking the essential question Who am I? and centered on a mission of helping people discover "The Real You." It's also not difficult to understand that being rejected and cut off from loved ones after devoting twelve years of her life to that same mission would leave Bornstein with complicated feelings.

Plus, Bornstein says that, in the church's eyes, she is classified as "Fair Game" and its members are permitted, even encouraged, to "destroy" her. High-ranking Scientologists dismiss the idea of Fair Game, calling it an unsubstantiated rumor of a long-dead policy, but there's proven evidence that it still exists. In the pro-logue to her memoir, Bornstein writes: "For over thirty years, I've been too afraid of the Church of Scientology to even try to mend bridges with my daughter. So, now I'm going to try. [. . .] And if they want to look, I'd like my daughter and grandchildren to see a few more dimensions in their dad and granddad."

Conquering her fear, accepting the risks, and hoping to start building the bridge to her daughter provided the impetus behind Bornstein's decision to write her memoir. "It's a big letter to her. That's what I wanted it to be," she explains. "And I wanted all the warts to show."

In her previous acclaimed and groundbreaking books, *Gender Outlaw*, *My Gender Workbook*, and *Hello, Cruel World*, Bornstein pioneered gender perspectives that made her a visible activist. "I'd always tried to go, push myself into saying more about myself, into revealing more, in pretty much all I've written." However, she says of *A Queer and Pleasant Danger*, "This required *everything*. And," she adds slyly, "that was a challenge enough to make it interesting to write."

Though the memoir was published in 2012, Bornstein really started it eight years earlier. She'd written an article called "Message in a Bottle" and sold it to *Salon* magazine. However, right before the article's publication, *Salon*'s lawyers warned them not to get involved because of potential repercussions from the Church of Scientology. The online magazine cancelled the article and gave Bornstein a kill fee. "I took it as the universe going, 'No, you're not ready to write this yet,'" she says. "I knew I would write something. That's what I do. But I knew I didn't have it a hundred percent right. I needed to get around the threat of writing about Scientology."

That threat was lifted when Bornstein got a little help from the creators of the satirical Comedy Central animated show *South Park*, who, in 2005, produced an episode called "Trapped in the Closet." Stan, a main character, joins Scientology and is thought to be the reincarnation of the church's founder, L. Ron Hubbard. The caption "This is what Scientologists actually believe" appeared on the screen throughout the program. "That broke the dam for a lot of this writing about [Scientology], and that made it much easier to write," Bornstein explains.

But, as Bornstein describes what the process of writing this deeply revealing material about the church and about herself was like, the word *easy* is not what springs to mind.

"I got terribly sick while writing it, all kinds of intestinal stuff—diverticulitis—and they had to take out close to a foot of intestine." She chuckles, saying that Louise Hay, the writer and motivational speaker who forged the philosophy of the mind-body connection, would have had a field day. "You know, it gets you right in your gut, and that's what writing this book was doing, and masochist that I am, I took that as a sign that I was on the right track. Hurts this much? Then I'm on the right track."

She's quiet for a moment and then says, "I don't like the writing. Do you?"

"The writing feels like labor for me a lot of the time," I reply. "But then there's a sense of satisfaction when I get to the end."

"Ah," she ponders. "You like *having written*. I love having written. I've written stuff easily, and none of it's been good."

"So how did you cope with the hard writing?" I ask.

Bornstein's answer is unexpected. "I binge-watched *Battlestar Galactica* and *Dr. Who* and re-watched all of *Buffy the Vampire Slayer*. I let myself have heroes, and I let myself fall into that." She laughs again. "I don't know that it was so much of an escape as, no matter how bad it was for me, it was worse for them. They're fending off aliens and vampires."

She also explains that at the time she was heavy into the writing, she had yet to address the borderline personality part of herself. "I was still flying off the handle or crashing terribly."

"What did that look like?" I ask.

She thinks about her answer for a moment and then says, "You know when you want to say something, and you don't know how to say it, and you can't stop trying to figure it out? It was that kind of worry, worry, think, think, think. Doing nothing—not eating, not really sleeping. Just typing crap onto document after document until you come up with the story that illustrates it all. Then you go, "Ah, fuck. There."

Carrellas helped Bornstein recognize that she needed help to deal with some of the symptoms that were emerging from the writing. "She basically said, 'Get thee to therapy.' And I did. I couldn't have done it without that."

Though Bornstein writes with what feels to the reader like fearless candor, and her own brand of self-effacing humor is intricately woven into her narrative, her memoir includes some darkly harrowing and disturbing scenes, among them painful memories of her relationship with her father and graphic descriptions of her practice of S&M.

She says that writing about her father in a way that didn't completely demonize him was the hardest part for her. A self-proclaimed male chauvinist pig, who, when Al Bornstein was only a teenager, set up a tryst for him with a prostitute to "make him a man," Paul Bornstein was often blatantly cruel. "It was just so much easier to do the one-dimensional bad guy, and coming up with and recalling loving moments, like where he sat me on his lap, that was hard. I remember stopping at that point and just going out for a walk. That was harder than pretty much any part." She stops speaking, and I can tell she's reflecting on her own words. "I don't know why," she finally says. "I haven't really looked at that. I just know that, again, it felt really good to have written that, but it was hell trying to get it out."

I broach the subject of the three-page S&M section in the memoir, a section she preludes with a trigger warning: "I'm going to give any reader an opportunity to skip over the hard parts. [. . .] If that's all you want to know, then please skip to the middle of page 218 and start with the sentence 'The WildRose Café was a lesbian coffeehouse . . . '" There are other descriptive sex scenes in the memoir, but I admit to Bornstein that this particular part of the book was difficult for me to read.

"Did you always know you'd include those parts in the book?" I ask. "Was that unrestrained kind of intimate exposure tough for you?"

"I've always been up front about my sadomasochism. It's fun because I know it's shocking. I like the shock factor a lot. That was part of the giggles in writing the book. So, no, that wasn't hard at all." The only hard part about it, she says, was thinking that her daughter and grandchildren might find those sections upsetting. The trigger warning was primarily written in deference to them.

We're interrupted by Carrellas opening the door and stepping into the room. With a resigned sigh, she states, "Another fucking shooting."

"What? Where?" Bornstein asks, sitting up on the edge of the bed. It's been less than a month since the brutal terrorist attacks in Paris, and the horror left in their wake is still raw.

"San Bernardino," Carrellas replies. She turns and walks out again. Later, we will learn that the shooting, at an agency that provides services for individuals with developmental disabilities, killed fourteen people. In the days ahead, these shootings will be linked to terrorism.

After Carrellas leaves, a sobering silence envelops us for a few moments. Then, Bornstein asks softly, "So what's more horrible? That? Or agreed-upon pain and pleasure?"

There's no argument to make.

"Let's back up to why I was able to write about these pieces of my life at all," Bornstein says, resetting the conversation. "Scientology." When she began writing regularly in the early 1990s, she'd been through her physical transition, but she still feared the Church of Scientology's power to come after her. "I knew that if I was self-revelatory to the point where I could say, 'Yeah, this is it, this is me; what are you going to do?' that there wasn't anything they could do to get me. So self-revelation to that degree was the cherry on top. It felt so good. I've said it all. Okay, done."

A Queer and Pleasant Danger is divided into three parts, and Bornstein summarizes the memoir's progression toward her full self-revelation this way: "The first part was all, 'Back then, back then, yah, yah, yah.' The second one was Scien-fucking-tology. And the third was . . ." She pauses and her voice quiets. "Candide, come home." Bornstein calls Voltaire's satirical novel "a touchstone for my life's telling." And it's obvious that the famous work influences the way Bornstein gives voice to her story—as a commanding presence who offers deep and enlightening reflection for her readers, but also whimsy and humor to soften the impact of some of the hard stuff.

"That's the part of having been in theater. You have to entertain an audience, and sometimes you have to make an audience cry." Bornstein explains that good theater allows moments of relief for the audience and that good memoir should do the same. "It's the principle of comfort food. Suddenly things are better and better, and they forgive you for making them cry."

The success of finishing the book was overshadowed by Bornstein's poor health at the time and her eventual lung cancer diagnosis. "I was sick every day. Every day, I was like, 'Oh my God, my gut. What's going on?' And after maybe two months on the road, I came back, and scan, scan, scan, scan—and aha."

Thinking back on finishing it now, though, Bornstein echoes many of the other memoirists in this book by noting the profound sense of relief she felt. "Starting all those years ago when I wrote the *Salon* article, really having decided to write about it and then this coming out, you go—'Ah, okay. It's out there.'"

Known to many in the queer community as "Auntie Kate" or "Granny Kate," Bornstein's authenticity in telling her story has given many of her followers, particularly kids struggling with their own gender identities, the courage to keep going. She's also been approached by ex-Scientologists and kids of ex-Scientologists who thank her for writing about her experience with the church. "I've been told that this has been encouraging and inspirational.

And good. That's good. I'm glad," she says, "because that makes it worth it."

According to Bornstein, the memoir has not gotten much press in the mainstream media. "It has only been reviewed in underground media, websites, LGBT sites, but no major outlets." She cracks a mischievous grin. "I think there're too many blow jobs."

"But," she goes on to say, "It's showing up in American literature classes that aren't LGBT. People think this is real literature, and that's a hoot. A major hoot. I thought it was going to be consigned to porn shops."

For Bornstein, a shadow still hangs over the positive response to her book. "When I finished writing it, I was for the first time able to say, 'I've done my duty as a father. I've done everything I can do; everything I know how to do.'" She stops, and a pained expression clouds her face. Disappointment weighs down her words. "Honestly, I think to myself, it didn't work. It hasn't worked because I haven't heard from my daughter or grandchildren."

"Do you think she's read it?" I ask.

"Of course she hasn't," Bornstein answers immediately. "She'd be thrown out if she read trash like this. But someone's going to see her and tell her that her dad wrote a book. That, I still believe. She may know I wrote a book; in which case, I hope the title makes her giggle."

When *A Queer and Pleasant Danger* came out and her cancer prognosis was murky, Bornstein did not expect to live long enough to see the end of 2015. Now, with her latest health updates, she intends to make her "extra alive-time," as she calls it, matter.

She's making plans. She's taking trips. She's promoting a new edition of *Gender Outlaw*. She also reveals that she was invited to be a regular cast member on Caitlyn Jenner's reality TV show, *I Am Cait*.

And, she hasn't given up on the possibility that maybe someday, somehow, she'll reconnect with her daughter.

For now, though, Bornstein settles for the consolation prize that in writing this memoir, she's presented herself to the rest of the world as sincerely as she knows how. "Tibetan Buddhists believe that eloquence is the telling of a truth in such a way that it eases suffering," she reflects. "That's eloquence. And the more suffering that is eased by your telling of the truth, the more eloquent you are. That's all you can really hope for—being eloquent in that fashion. All you have to do is respond to your story honestly, and that's the ideal."

CHAPTER 15

Jessica Handler

· *Invisible Sisters*
· *Braving the Fire: A Guide
to Writing about Grief and Loss*

It's appropriate that to find the entrance to a restaurant called Hell's Kitchen, I have to weave down a set of long stairs to a subterranean space beneath Minneapolis' bustling city streets. Crimson walls trimmed in black form the backdrop for eclectic pieces of gothic décor, including a mounted minotaur-like skull, chandeliers dangling knives and meat cleavers, a tree inhabited by stuffed vultures, and Ralph Steadman prints depicting grotesque images distorted by spattered ink. Whether morbid or ironic or strikingly fitting, maybe a subtle mix of all three, this is where I'm meeting author Jessica Handler to learn about her process in writing her memoir, *Invisible Sisters*, her courageous story of profound loss, and how that process spawned *Braving the Fire*, her craft guide to writing about grief.

On this drizzly and cold Friday morning in April, Handler and I meet midway through the 2015 Association of Writers and Writing Programs Convention that we and about twelve thousand others have descended on Minnesota's "City of Lakes" to attend.

Handler, a tall woman in her middle fifties, her gray hair cut in a short, no-fuss, spiky style, waits at the bottom of the stairs and greets me with a wide smile. Marianne Leone introduced us via e-mail, and Handler and I have chatted on the phone and exchanged some messages. Similar to so many of my other first in-person encounters with the authors I've profiled, the threads of our shared experience make Handler feel familiar. Later in our conversation, Handler will name this feeling: "You and I, and everybody you are talking to for this book, we're all members of the same tribe." It's not a tribe any of us asked to be a part of, but the more of its people I meet, the more grateful I feel to be welcomed in.

We follow the hostess to a cozy booth next to the bar. "I've heard great things about the food here," Handler says. I love a good breakfast, and when our server brings my plate stacked with scrambled eggs, home fries, and two slices of thick-crusted sourdough toast, I do dive in. It's into Handler's story, though, that I really want to dive, and I'm excited to get the conversation going.

I explain the background of my project. "As the book is taking shape, I'm realizing that a lot of what I'm asking each author is new territory. In so many interviews I've read, the interviewers seem almost intent on ignoring the profound emotion that goes into writing these kinds of trauma memoirs."

"That's the hardest part," Handler says, shaking hot sauce onto her eggs from one of the three different bottles with varying degrees of heat that had accompanied our meals. "Anybody can talk to you about craft techniques, but by asking me, 'How did you do it?' I can give you moments of crying; I can give you moments of laughter; I can give you terror; I can give you thoughts about the box on my shelf that I don't look at. You are asking good questions."

Her faith shouldn't surprise me. Handler understands that sometimes in this writing life, all we want to know is how other writers have made it through and what they did to cope along the way. It's why she penned her second book, *Braving the Fire: A Guide to Writing About Grief and Loss.* In its introduction she writes: "I was desperate for good books that proved that I wasn't alone in the journey my family and I had made: a journey that left me as the surviving sister of three. [. . .] I was searching for a roadmap to understanding my grief, and eventually, how to write well about it." Using the structure of Elisabeth Kubler-Ross's five stages of grief—denial, anger, bargaining, depression, acceptance—and then adding a sixth stage of her own—renewal—Handler offers her personal testimony with accompanying interview excerpts from other authors who've written about grief. Each chapter ends with exercises she's used in her teaching of memoir to help the writer kick-start the process of examining and shaping the grief experience.

Handler sees the Kubler-Ross stages as "useful scaffolding" for someone approaching the grief writing process, but not a formula. "I can't tell anybody how they 'have' to do it, in the same way you can't tell anybody how their grieving is right or wrong. It's different for everybody. Don't abuse anybody and don't abuse yourself, but beyond that there's no right or wrong. There's going to be flinching. Pain. You don't want to go there, yet you need to go there."

Many of Handler's *Braving the Fire* readers have expressed the following sentiment about being encouraged to "go there": "Thank you for the way in." That "way in" is what I've needed in my writing process. I also express my gratitude to Handler for writing *Braving the Fire*. I've benefitted from its wise insights in crafting my memoir.

Handler smiles. "I'm glad it is helpful. That's what I need to hear. Was I just hollerin' down a hole, or was it helpful?" The South has snuck into her dialect and her accent. Until now, I've heard only traces of her Georgia twang. Though she lives with her husband, Mickey Dubrow, in Atlanta and spent most of her childhood and teen years in Georgia, Handler had periods of living on both the West and East coasts. This regional hop-scotching enables her to unconsciously temper her speech depending on her locale, making her accent more generic.

Writing about her Georgia childhood and her family's heart-breaking story of grief and loss is the personal fire that Handler had to brave so she could offer others helpful tools to venture into their own stories of grief. The product of Handler's courageous journey is her deeply moving memoir, *Invisible Sisters*.

Handler is the oldest of three sisters. In a cruel irony, her younger sisters both endured diseases whose courses are determined by the number of white blood cells the body produces. At six years old, Handler's sister, Susie, developed acute lymphocytic leukemia—a blood cancer that generates too many white blood cells—and died two years later. Handler's second sister, Sarah, was born with Kostmann's syndrome—a rare genetic disorder that left her body without enough white blood cells to fight infection—and died at twenty-seven. "Sarah lived about twenty-five years longer than expectations," Handler explains.

With Sarah's death in 1992, Handler became, at thirty-two, "the only one left." In an effort to understand that identity, and the long trail of events leading to it, Handler began writing *Invisible Sisters*, asking, "What does it mean to be the last one standing?"

The common query, "Do you have any brothers or sisters?"—a question she still struggles to know how to answer—was the catalyst for writing about her experiences. "In my late thirties, forties, I needed to explain to myself what happened. I missed my family, and I needed to look at them and understand who we were and who we could have been. That's the painful thing, who you could have been."

Like so many of the other writers I've spoken to, Handler tried to write her story as fiction first, but soon discovered, as they did, that fiction could not do the story justice. "It just didn't work, but I kept trying to write about it." She attended the Iowa Summer Writers Workshop with an essay called "Take Three Eggs," a reference to a recipe but also to three eggs, three babies. Her workshop readers told her, "This is a story that matters."

Handler decided to pursue an MFA at Queens University of Charlotte, in North Carolina. Her thesis work eventually became

Invisible Sisters. "It went through many revisions." She points to my copy on the table and chuckles. "I'd call that 'Thesis Version 8.0.'"

Handler begins each chapter with an epigraph pulled from family artifacts—letters, medical records, newspaper clippings. These snippets of history are an affecting draw for readers. Many are her own words from journals she's kept since she was nine years old. "I didn't think of myself as a memory keeper overtly as a kid. I come from a very literary family, a very word-driven family, and I just always wrote."

These and the other relics Handler's collected were her "way in" to her own story. They also forced her to confront some of the difficult questions that haunted her, including the earlier mention of the box on her shelf that she doesn't look at. In *Braving the Fire*, Handler writes about a battered cardboard crate containing Sarah's journals that Handler has never read. "I have a tote bag of some of Sarah's clothing too. I still have it in the attic. Sarah was five feet tall. I'm five foot eight. There's no way I could wear them. But I have them." She laughs. "I'm not a hoarder, but I think I'm keeping these artifacts because I don't have the people." Her voice softens. "Which isn't the same. How do I tell myself what I'm doing with this stuff? And also how do I tell the world about these people who I loved?"

By finally engaging with these questions and seeking to answer them, Handler found her story's scaffolding. "The book just sort of emerged."

Invisible Sisters does not gloss over the experience of loss. Handler takes her reader into the anguish that infiltrated her home after Susie's death—anguish no one talked about, that transformed her father into an addict coming apart at the seams and made her mother someone who modeled that pain was something to be borne silently. Stifling her grief and the ongoing fear of the eventuality of Sarah's death, Handler turned inward. She writes, "What I wanted to do was scream, but our family code required silence about dire emotion. Instead, I opened my mouth wide and learned to scream without making a sound."

"What was it like for you to finally give words to those emotions?"

"It became more of a book and less of a scream," she replies. That shift took time. Handler had to give herself permission to be honest. Honest about things like the destructive behavior she observed in her father as a coping mechanism for his grief. Honest about the destructive behavior she spent a period of her early adulthood embroiled in to cope with her own.

"Do you think seeing your father basically go off the rails gave you license to do the same?"

She's thoughtful. "I bet. Not until you said it, but you are right. Seeing that Dad could spring a leak, basically let me know that I could spring a leak too."

Writing honestly was not easy for Handler. "I often felt like, 'I can't talk about this.'" But it wasn't just about exposing family truths. There was stigma, too. "In the larger world, we didn't talk about it, partly because people backed away. People didn't like to talk about cancer then. They sure as shit didn't like to talk about pediatric cancer. Now, because of Facebook, people are always raising money for bald kids. . . ." She pauses and swallows hard. "I still cannot look at bald kids," she confesses, and I can see on her face the pain of images that must still be etched in her psyche. She describes trying to watch the PBS film *Emperor of All Maladies*, based on the Pulitzer Prize winner by Siddhartha Mukherjee, a book Handler loves. "I get one look at a bald child and the visceral reaction makes me want to pick the television up and hurl it out the window. That has something to do with PTSD, but it also has something to do with not talking about it."

Handler recognized she needed to talk. "It was almost like I said, 'All right, here I'm going to tell it. I'm just going to lay it out and see what I see.'"

"Did you tell anyone in your family you were writing the story?"

"My father had died by then, and so it was just my mom. My mother was a magazine editor throughout her career, and I'd talk about the book as I was writing, and sometimes we'd compare memories. It was very enlightening for her to see what she remembered as a mother, I remembered from the point of view of an eight-year-old, a fifteen-year-old, and that our losses were the same and very different."

Handler asks me if I've shown any of my manuscript to my family. "Not yet," I reply. "I don't know how they'll react."

"Your brothers' points of view, your mother's point of view—same way with my mother and me about Sarah or about Susie—the facts are the same, but her perception was this, my perception was that. That's all there is. Your mother and brothers may be sad about things you're not sad about. That'll be kind of interesting to see." I'm reminded of my conversation with Andre Dubus III. "That's what happens with memoir—certainly with trauma memoir. It's an act of understanding and an act of bridging. And I don't want to get all "Kumbaya" about it, but there is an act of saying, 'Now, I get it.'"

"Were there moments when you wondered if you should be writing it?"

"I did converse with Sarah in my head a little bit," Handler admits. "And there were times when I could almost hear her saying, 'You are not going to tell that!'"

Handler also remembers a particularly revealing moment with her mother. "She said, 'Why are you writing this? People don't want to know this.' I said, 'They do, and I want to know it.' But it made me feel badly for her because I know that her whole life as the mother of these children and the wife of this man was so devoted to keeping us together, making things as right as they could be in the face of things that cannot be made right. So when she said, 'Nobody's interested,' I knew that was her patting down the edges. Making hospital corners on the bed."

As the book took shape, Handler intentionally chose to leave pieces of the story out. "I'd write them and I'd realize, you know what? That's me inventing. Or, it doesn't support the narrative. I know that's a craft thing to say, but it's also me saying I don't need to tell everything because I don't want to and because it detracts from what I'm trying to do emotionally, intellectually, culturally."

"How did it feel to finish?"

"Stunning," she responds immediately. "Not because, 'Oh, I wrote a book, I'm going to be famous' because I'm not. But," her voice shakes a little with the weight of her next words, "I felt like I had done right by my sisters."

Invisible Sisters was named Best Memoir of 2009 by *Atlanta Magazine* and the Georgia Center for the Book named it one of the "25 Books All Georgians Should Read." It would be a disservice to Handler and her story to isolate its value to one locale, though. Any reader anywhere who has been touched by grief or loss will benefit from her candor and wisdom.

Handler's memoir cleared a path for her readers to speak about their unspeakable losses. "I got a lot of letters from people thanking me or saying, 'I'm the only one left too.' Or 'Your story makes me realize I can talk about mine.' I found other people like me too." People who could identify with the complexities of her loss. "I had dinner last night with two women who are sisters," she says. "I enjoyed them and they were fabulous, but they were teasing each other, and there's a little part of me that is inside having a tantrum. I imagine you feel that way about people and their dads. We are angry. We will always be angry and heartbroken."

Writing *Invisible Sisters* and seeing it in print created a shift in Handler's anger and heartbreak. "I wasn't as afraid of it. I wasn't as afraid of crying. I mean, right now I'm talking to you. I'm drinking a cup of coffee. I have on eyeliner. But at the same time, inside me, I want to just put my head on this nice table and cry until I throw up. And I can acknowledge that now." Before, she would have buried it and claimed she was fine. "I tell this to my students all the time when I'm teaching trauma writing. It doesn't mean that I don't miss my sisters. It doesn't mean that I don't love them. It doesn't mean that a part of me isn't on this sublevel, this sort of low hum of almost consistent freaking out. It's just that now I know that it is a part of my life."

Handler circles back to the idea of writing our stories as an act of bridging. "Everybody's story is different. The facts, the situations of my loss are not the same as Mark Doty's, they're not the same as Chris Cooper's and Marianne Leone's, they're not the same as yours. But fundamentally the way we are changed and the way we look at ourselves and our surroundings, that's where the similarity is. That's where the connection is."

I feel a twinge of regret when I reach my last question. Like so many of the others I've had, I don't want this conversation to end. "Can you tell me what was most surprising about this entire journey for you?"

"You don't get rid of the story," Handler begins after a minute. "Writing the book made the story something that I can integrate. Isn't that weird? You take it out of yourself and look at it so that you can reintegrate it and move forward."

Before we say our good-byes, Handler pulls back the sleeve of her sweater and shows me the inside of her right wrist. Three lines are tattooed across her skin in black, typewriter script: *The door itself makes no promises. It is only a door.*

"It's the last stanza of Adrienne Rich's poem, 'Prospective Immigrants Please Note.' I wish now I'd gotten the whole poem, but at fifty-five, I'm a little old to have a full tattoo sleeve," Handler laughs. "But isn't that the essence of all of this," she says meeting my eyes. "You make your choices. You take your chances. You go into something. You don't know what you are going to get, but you make the step."

CHAPTER 16

Richard Blanco

· *The Prince of Los Cocuyos: A Miami Childhood*

On January 21, 2013, a day marked by all the pomp and ceremony the United States has to offer, poet Richard Blanco, dressed in a black wool overcoat—a crisp white shirt and navy-blue tie visible beneath—rose from his seat beside his mother on a packed stage at the West Front of the US Capitol that overlooked a crowd of hundreds of thousands of people gathered on the National Mall in Washington, DC, and did something only four others in the history of the country had ever done. He stood at a podium bearing the seal of the president of the United States, smiled, long dimples creasing his cheeks, opened a heavy blue folder, took two quick breaths, and then, with a poise that did not betray his nerves, flawlessly read his poem, "One Today," composed for the occasion of President Barack Obama's second inauguration.

Blanco, the youngest and first Latino, immigrant, and openly gay person to be chosen for the honor, did not realize the full breadth and reach of that one moment when he returned to his seat seven minutes later amidst a deafening standing ovation. In what he calls his "memoirette," *For All of Us, One Today: An Inaugural Poet's Journey*, a concise narrative that begins with the call that gave him the news he'd been chosen as inaugural poet and traces the uncharted path that led him to that stage, Blanco writes: "For the most part, poets live and write contentedly inside the circle of literati and academics, myself included. Accustomed to that kind of relative obscurity, I naively thought I'd simply read my poem, shake a few hands, get back home, and that would be that."

He didn't know then that the power of his poem's message, cradled in the beauty of his words, heard by millions worldwide, would launch him to an immediate position of notoriety. He didn't know then that over the next three years, he would leave his day job as a civil engineer; would have the opportunity as a speaker, teacher, and writer to again and again engage diverse audiences in the United States and around the world through the ongoing artistic outlet of his poetry; and would in a few pivotal circumstances, including the reading of his occasional poem "Boston Strong" at a benefit concert on May 30, 2013, following the Boston Marathon bombings, speak words that provide much-needed salve on raw, emotional wounds.

And Blanco didn't know then that his second memoir, *The Prince of Los Cocuyos: A Miami Childhood*, the often funny, always intimate, and profoundly moving reminiscence of his bewildering boyhood and adolescent years as the son of Cuban immigrants, searching for his place in this world at the intersections of his cultural, sexual, and creative identities, would speak so powerfully to a diverse collection of readers, including me. Nor did he know that on a frigid afternoon in the middle of February 2016, he'd end up in the Saltbox Kitchen, a farm-to-table cafe in Concord, Massachusetts, talking about how the book came to be.

Only a few hours earlier, Blanco had returned from a trip to DC. On my drive in, I'd heard White House press secretary Josh Earnest announce that both the president and first lady would be traveling to Cuba in March—a historic visit that would be the first of its kind in eighty-eight years—and I'd wondered if Blanco's trip to Washington was related. "I was actually there for a totally different reason," Blanco tells me after ordering a strong coffee and pulling up a gray, spindle-back chair to the weathered barn-board table next to the windows. His voice is deep and a little hoarse with the fatigue of travel and the smoky remains of the cigarette he'd finished before walking through the door. I don't press him for further details of his trip. That's not why we're here.

Instead, I ask Blanco to tell me what made him, an acclaimed poet, venture into the land of memoir. "In part, it was sort of creative curiosity to begin with," he explains. "My third book of poetry had been accepted, and I thought, well what do I want to do next?" He grins, and I again notice his dimpled cheeks. "Nobody was waiting for my fourth book of poetry."

A sense of personal challenge also fueled Blanco's decision to try writing in a new genre. "I had scars from my MFA days, of handing in manuscripts for required prose classes and hearing, 'This is beautiful, but nothing happens!' I just wanted to learn."

Writing about his childhood in Miami and the shaping of his cultural and sexual identities was nothing new for Blanco. He'd explored a lot of that material in his earlier poetry collections. "But there was a backlog of memories and stories and anecdotes for which poetry was never the right vehicle. So, I started exploring and looking at what my life would look like without line breaks."

Similar to what poets Mark Doty and Richard Hoffman discovered when they first began writing prose, Blanco found unexpected freedom in the open space of the genre. "There was a way of expanding on some of the characters and family members and experiences, and I just sort of got hooked in that sense. In some ways, the memoir of my Miami childhood is really the first half of my first book of poetry unpacked."

Blanco began with essays, and though he knew he always wanted a book, he thought it would look more like a collection. "The essays were really just a prelude to the memoir. I used them or recycled them in some ways—there was some thinking going on there that was help for the memoir." The essayistic structure lingers in the book. Divided into seven chapters, each centering on a particular relationship from his childhood, the story has a clear chronology and narrative arc, but there's also a sense of containment in each chapter, so each episode from Blanco's life could stand on its own.

"What did it feel like for you as you started to see those childhood memories taking that more expanded form?"

"The memoir was easier to write on some levels because some of the emotional work had already been done. I realized I work out my things emotionally in my poetry, so I kind of knew what was the emotional core of some of the stories I wanted to tell."

For the first time, though, Blanco did feel some hesitation in telling some of these stories. He laughs and says that until writing the memoir, he'd never understood why people might be afraid to write about things. "I was like, 'What do you mean you're scared?' My family doesn't read English—at least the elders—and so with my poetry, I never really thought about it much because the chances of my poetry being translated into Spanish were slim. My parents weren't going to read the stuff." He'd been somewhat naïve, he admits. "This was a very different case because I was not only writing something that I thought could be translated, but, also, I was writing about other generations of my Cuban American family—like my cousins and my brother—that do read English."

Taking on the challenge of the memoir and writing with a consciousness of what to say and what not to say was totally new. "I'm not revealing any deep dark family secrets," Blanco qualifies, "but there were moments when I had to go back and look at things, at characters." His older brother, Carlos, was one of those characters. "In the first draft, my brother comes across as a complete pain in the butt." Blanco chuckles. "I had to shift that as I realized there was partial liability on both sides. Both of us were at it all the time. We were both brats."

Another unanticipated worry Blanco bumped into was his portrayal of Miami. "In this book the city is a character or, no, the experience of the city is a character, I should say. I was writing knowing that there were people reading this book, Miamians, people that lived in Westchester [the area of Miami where Blanco grew up], that were going to scrutinize it." He conducted a lot of "weird digital research" to make sure he had specific details of place right. "I was afraid of a virtual character, and that was really surprising to me."

Along the way, Blanco planted some guideposts that would help to ease some of those writing fears. "I had to keep the ghosts out of the room. They could come on the page, but not in the room." Blanco also accepted that there are no hard and fast rules to memoir. "I gave myself liberty to sort of engage this as a poet. And the contract with myself and with my readers was that of a poem. I kept the principle of emotional truth."

That principle permitted Blanco to use techniques of poetry in the narrative. "I'm pulling images. I'm coalescing memories and distilling and embroidering them into one story, which is what you do with a poem." He expands on this idea in his author's note at the beginning of *The Prince of Los Cocuyos*: "I've bent time and space in the way that the art of memory demands. My poet's soul believes that the emotional truth of these pages trumps everything. Read as you would read my poems, trusting that what is here is real, beyond what is real—that truer truth which we come to call a life."

Blanco took time to research how other memoirists had solved this problem of memory and truth. "There are some really bold author notes in a lot of memoirs ranging from: 'Everything here is completely true except these two things' to 'I don't care what you think is true or not.' I just wanted to be forthright with the reader and say, 'I don't want any problems here.'"

The emotional truths of Blanco's poetry and the emotional truths of his prose did exhibit some stark contrasts—especially when it came to the representation of some of the pivotal people in his life. "The one character I couldn't get close to was my father, and in the narrative, he's kind of like a ghost because that's the way he was. Unlike in the poetry, where you can make a powerful poem about that silence, in the memoir, if nothing happens, then there's just nothing to tell." Blanco's relationship with his father had to be defined in the subtext. That his father is not a principal character throughout the book tells the reader that story without needing to tell it.

Blanco uncovered another startling contrast. "I had written poetry about my grandmother and my mother. In my poetry, my mother is revered as this sort of martyr, because I'm zeroing in on her soul, which is what a poem does, and connecting with her loss and suffering over having to leave her entire family in Cuba. And in my poetry I'm much more vicious with my grandmother, because I'm looking at her dark side. In the memoir, which surprised the hell out of me, my mother comes across as this control-freak, complete neurotic mess—and she was; I realized she was. The memoir dealt with the exterior character first. And then my grandmother, on the surface, was like a cross between Napoleon and Billy Crystal. Everybody loved her."

Blanco's tone shifts, a somber note playing through his words. "But nobody saw her behind closed doors. The verbal abuse. She was really dark at times." "Dark" seems a kinder word than I would choose for the often hateful and repressive ways Blanco's homophobic grandmother expressed her fears that he may not be joining the ranks of the "manly men," *los hombres*. The challenge for Blanco was to represent the full dimensions of these characters on the page. "You have to dig deeper."

Digging deeper also meant unearthing some painful memories that Blanco had not looked at before. One such heartache is the tragic death of one of his closest friends, a character he calls Julio, when Blanco is fifteen years old. "I had never written about him. Tears flowed. I had never processed that part of my life. Who understands death at fifteen? I realized that at that age, you don't know what to do with that. You just sort of went on the next day, went through the motions, but sort of swept everything under the rug." He pauses for a moment. "Now, I realize how all those years I had been thinking about him and how it had affected me and what I think about life. I mourned his death in those two chapters where he appears."

"How did you keep writing through that grief?"

"I should say that I'm a sentimental fool. And, I think in the context of what you are writing about and investigating for this book, poets have probably an easier time with memoir because we are used to going there. In fact, I don't think a poem is a poem until I'm crying. Then I know a poem is done, or at least, I've hit something. I've hit a nerve." Blanco circles back to writing about his sorrow over Julio's death. "I actually wanted to get to that point. I would just write right through it. My poetic instincts just took over. In a way, it thrills me to be in touch with that raw emotion. And I wasn't expecting that in memoir."

Blanco's eyes are wet at the corners, and his voice catches. "It wasn't only about his death. It was something colored over the years by memory, so it was also a process of bringing him back to life." His voice is filled with such tenderness and the same emotion is mirrored on his face when he says, "I'm getting misty talking about it right now, but resurrecting him made me realize he was my best friend. I never really acknowledged that, and that's what made me sentimental too. That sense that I had one friend at least. He was the one person I could always be myself around. So it was a painful process of bringing him to life and then killing him."

The other central piece of the book that Blanco had never really dealt with was how he felt about his sexuality through high school. "That was emotional in a different way—not in a crying kind of way, but in a very complex, mind-boggling sort of way. You realize that you have no language at that age to process." Blanco explains that at that time in his world, there was no guide-book for a young gay man. "I had no gay role models. There was no National Coming Out Day. No, 'It Gets Better Project.'" At his all-boys Catholic high school, Blanco felt isolated and lonely. "I was walking around in this sort of virtual reality all the time. You know the truth in your heart is there, but you don't have language for it."

The conundrum in writing about those feelings, Blanco continues, is "How do you as a narrator explain with language that you have no language? The best language I found was 'a knowing without knowing.' The rest had to be gestures or episodes of things."

To go to those moments and dig into his psyche at the time, Blanco says there was a sense of abstracting himself in the same way he often does with poetry. "We have a persona. I think of myself as a third-person character and in my notes I write, 'What did Little Riqui feel at that moment?' I refer to everything in third person." That abstraction can also be hard. "I'd pull out a memory and it's like going back to being a seven-year-old, but I'm thinking about it as a forty-seven–year-old, so when I write about the memory, I'm doing so with the reflections of an adult in present time."

Another, more established shield for Blanco in the writing process was that many of the difficult characters he had to write about were no longer living. "Even in the poetry, I never wrote about my grandmother until she died. I'm not sure I did that consciously; I just think I wasn't ready to process it all. So, when I wrote the book, my father had died, my grandfather had died, my grandmother had died." Blanco grins and says, "It's a lot easier to write after everybody dies."

Despite many of the serious topics we discuss, there's a lot of laughter in my conversation with Blanco. He's one of those people who easily engage with humor, possessing the kind of natural wit that cannot be taught. That same trait is woven into the narrative voice of his memoir, making for many laugh-out-loud moments to provide balance to the more tender, and sometimes heartbreaking, scenes.

"Did you know that humor was going to be one of the vehicles you'd use to tell this story?" I ask Blanco now.

"I think so," he replies. "Not completely consciously, but humor is a cultural characteristic. It's a reflection of the sensibility of the very people and the very experiences I was writing about—a tragic/comic sense of life that is so Latino and so Cuban, in particular. You're laughing one moment and crying the next. I knew I wanted that to be part of the texture of the book." Blanco expands on the thought, "People think Latinos are emotional, but there's a difference between being emotional and dramatic. We're often dramatic to hide emotions. Everything turns into this drama, but we're not really talking about what we need to talk about. There's a comedy of errors in there somewhere. I mean, I thought I had a normal grandmother all my life. I thought everybody's grandmother calls their grandson 'faggot,' you know?" The not really talking about things made Little Riqui believe that's just the way life was.

"You go back through those details because the art is demanding that honesty, demanding that you look, and look, and look, and look. And then you form a narrative around it, and the narrative has to have a beginning, a middle, and end, and you realize there is an arc to your life that you never recognized before. Writing lets us close those chapters in a way." Blanco reflects for a few seconds before continuing. "Very few people take the time to go back and heal that child or give them a pat on the back or say it's going to be all right. We spend all of our lives without ever really examining our past, our lives." He gives me a knowing smile. "Unless, of course, we write a memoir. It's either that or therapy. But even therapy can't compare to writing a memoir. One memoir is about ten years' worth of therapy!"

Though Blanco ends his memoir at a fixed threshold in his life—the summer before his final year of high school—he flashes forward to what he refers to in the book as "all my somedays," beautiful revelations of what the future holds for Little Riqui. "It was like I gave him a pat on the back and said, 'It is going to be okay.'" Blanco's eyes fill again, and he softly says, "I wished someone had been there to do that for me."

Finishing the memoir was a bit of a jarring experience for Blanco. "I was originally writing it here and there and thinking someday, maybe a memoir. I was just having fun." There's no arrogance in Blanco's next words; he simply states the facts. "Then the inauguration happened, and all that attention and exposure led to a scramble of agents calling and selling it, so the process of getting it finished got really accelerated."

Blanco is honest about wishing he'd had a little more space to work on it, but recognizes that the scramble did push him to get the book done. "I really didn't have time to sort of savor it. I turned the thing in, and it was like business." But then, he says, the book arrived in the mail, and a huge sense of accomplishment that he'd written the story really set in. As did a profound sense of closure. "You know how they say that everybody's always writing one poem or one story or one novel all their lives? My childhood has always been this magical world because everything was so wonderfully weird and confusing. The memoir let me put those years somewhere, and at this point, I don't need to dive anymore into my childhood in the same way. I'm still obsessed with the idea of home, but it's more global, philosophical."

Since its publication in 2014, *The Prince of Los Cocuyos* has received rave editorial reviews. In 2015, it won the Lambda Literary Award for Best Gay Memoir and was selected for common-read programs at several schools. Along with the critical praise, Blanco's memoir has also reconnected him to important people from his past.

"A lot of people from the neighborhood, Westchester, a lot of people from grade school, have reached out to me. Even though they're not in the book per se, they're so honored that someone wrote about our lives. We think our lives are sort of these plain, ordinary things, and they suddenly realized the specialness of what we shared. Everybody was so proud that somebody wrote about Miami and that particular perspective of that particular decade."

One beautiful reunion happened with his fourth-grade teacher—a character who plays a relatively minor role in the book, but who'd had a lasting impact on Blanco's life. "She was one of the few people that were there for me, someone I held close," he reflects. After the inauguration, they got in touch with each other, and when Blanco was slated to do a reading in her hometown of Mobile, Alabama, he invited her to come. "She was exactly how

I remembered her. She was heartbroken by my story, especially what I was going through with my grandmother. She said, 'I feel like I failed you; I feel like I didn't protect you.' And I'm like, 'Are you kidding? If it wasn't for you, I wouldn't have made it to the fifth grade!'" She also gave him her manuscript to look at. "The student became the teacher and the teacher became the student. It was so emotional."

That younger generation of Blanco's Cuban American family that he'd worried about in the beginning—his brother and cousins—expressed only positive reactions to the memoir. He says his mother, though, has never mentioned it to him. "All she's ever told me in jest is that she should get royalties for all the inspiration that she's given me." He's uncertain whether she's read it, but he knows she's aware of what's in it. "She's also a shielded person in a way and doesn't dig too deep. Some people don't want to dive back in."

Blanco also relates some reactions he wasn't anticipating. "I didn't expect how ethnic literature becomes this genre by itself. A lot of people were like, 'I'm going to buy this for my neighbor who's Cuban or my brother-in-law who's Cuban.' They say it as a compliment, but it's as idiotic as saying, 'I'm going to buy this Robert Frost book because I have a friend who lives in New England. I'm going to buy Doctor Zhivago because I have a friend who lives in Russia.' It was like, 'I can't own this book because I'm not Cuban.' Even though they'd probably get more out of the book than Cubans. Cubans already know the story in a way."

The finality Blanco felt at the end of writing a memoir was another contrast to his poetry. "You don't go back and reread fiction or memoir very often, but you do with poetry because it doesn't have that same finality. You always find something else." For a while, that sensation made Blanco want to go back and do more with the book, or write a follow-up to what has been classified as his "cultural coming of age" story. But then he asked himself, "When do we ever stop becoming? We're always coming of age in many, many complex ways. We have a million unfinished chapters in our lives."

The fundamental value of the journey has gone much deeper than the simple telling of a childhood story, Blanco reflects as our interview comes to a close. "To write a poem, a book, is one of the stupidest, most self-serving, dumb, arrogant, selfish things anybody can be doing in the world," he says, throwing back his head and laughing. But then he adds, "And yet it's one of the most selfless, most giving, most gregarious, most adoring things anybody can do in this world. I'm not writing the book just for me. I'm ultimately writing that book for someone else to see themselves in that book. In the same way that people gift us words that help us, we pass on that gift as writers. We pass on that gift for others to see something about their lives that they had never seen and maybe to go to places that they need to go even if it hurts. The greatest compliment anybody can give me is, 'Your book made me think of a time when I . . . fill in the blank.'"

My mind travels back to Blanco's inaugural poem and its final words, uniting all of us "under one sky." How he speaks of *hope* as "a new constellation waiting for us to map it, waiting for us to name it—together."

I hear echoes of those themes now in his last words to me. "At the end of all this, why we endeavor collectively to write a book or paint a canvas or write a symphony or whatnot, is to understand who we are as human beings, and it's that shared knowledge that somehow helps us to survive."

CHAPTER 17

Alysia Abbott

· *Fairyland: A Memoir of My Father*

The late June day I visit author Alysia Abbott in her Cambridge, Massachusetts, home happens to be the last day of school both for her children and for mine. As she leads me up the flight of stairs from the entryway to her second floor, the space occupied by her main living area—an open-concept kitchen, dining, and living room flooded with natural light—she tells me that the soundtrack she'd chosen to accompany breakfast for her daughter, Annabel, and son, Finn, included Alice Cooper's "School's Out" and ELO's "I'm Alive." I listen to her description of this send-off and can't help but think that for someone who grew up without her own mother, Abbott seems to be getting the mothering thing pretty right.

Abbott, a beautiful woman in her middle forties, carries her personal style, modish and bohemian, with an effortless confidence. Today, she's relaxed in a plain t-shirt and cargo pants, her dark hair pulled back loosely in a clip, black-rimmed glasses framing her large brown eyes, red lipstick the only trace of makeup on her face. We settle in the scoop-back chairs at her dining table to begin our conversation, and I feel the shared fragments of our experiences putting me at ease. We are both mothers. Both writers. Both teachers. And we are both daughters who lost beloved fathers way too soon to the same devastating and deeply misunderstood disease.

I'd first met Abbott a few months earlier at the 2015 AWP conference in Minneapolis when I'd attended her presentation on bringing the larger cultural and historical contexts of the world into our personal stories. Abbott's exquisite book, *Fairyland: A Memoir of My Father*, explores the social and political landscapes that enveloped her intimate story of growing up with writer and poet Steve Abbott, her single, gay father, in 1970s San Francisco, living through the tumultuous height of the AIDS crisis in the 1980s, and losing her father to AIDS in 1992. Her talk resonated at a particularly personal level for me, so when I approached her after the panel discussion, my emotions felt unusually charged. I'd prepared a whole speech in my head about her book and her presentation, but when I'd gotten my chance to speak, I only said that my father also died of AIDS. Then, I'd thrust a chapter of my memoir into her hands and literally ran away. Not one of my finest moments. When I e-mailed her a few weeks later to follow up with an apology for my lack of poise, she invited me to meet her for lunch in Boston, and it was then that we had the chance to talk through some of the intersections in our stories. I asked her if we could meet again so I could learn more about the making of *Fairyland*, and this time she invited me to her home.

"Because my father was a writer, and I had always had intentions and hopes to be a writer myself, I think I considered, even when he was living, writing about us," Abbott begins when I ask her what made her start writing about the life she'd lived with her dad. "There was always this idea."

Abbott had a compelling story to tell. When her mother died in a car crash, Abbott was only three. Her father, who'd come out before his wife died and before Abbott was born, moved himself and his young daughter to San Francisco, where she grew up immersed in the artistic and literary scenes at the heart of one of the country's largest and most liberated gay communities. Abbott also lived through the decimation that HIV/AIDS carved through this community and the responsibility of caring for her own dying father before his death from AIDS-related complications.

Abbott knew from the beginning that she had both the tools and resources to write this book. "I'd saved all the letters that my dad wrote me, and he'd saved the letters I wrote him when I was in college. One of the first things I did was to put them in order and put them in plastic sleeves so I could read them. These letters had so much of my father's voice and energy in them, and [writing] was a way of keeping that alive."

Abbott also had an abundant store of her father's other writings—poetry, diaries, cartoons—writing that portrayed his professional career, what he'd lived through, and what her life had been like long before her own memory gathered the experiences. "His life was just fascinating to me, and I knew that I was the only one who was going to really be able to tell this story." Writing the book that tells this story, though, was something that Abbott would circle for twenty years before publishing *Fairyland*.

"There was an emotional reserve to my first attempts to write about us," she muses as she reflects on an initial piece she wrote for her father's memorial service. "It felt kind of distant, and it was very, very hard for me." The grief of the loss was still too raw. "Even when I was living with him, I had a journal, but I could never really write in the journal because in a way it was just too painful what was going on, and I needed to spend more of my time sort of getting away from it and not trying to get into it more."

After her father died, Abbott moved back to New York City, where she'd been living and going to school before she'd gone to San Francisco to care for him when he was too sick to care for himself. She took some adult education classes and tried again to write her way into their story. "The memories were still fresh, so I was able to write in some detail about the smell and feeling of things like his bedroom, the room where he spent his final months, and what the room was like." She's matter-of-fact in the telling, but when she pauses to gather her thoughts, the depth of these memories is present in the distant look that crosses her face. "It was very emotional, and I would sort of write these felt scenes, but without any context or story. They meant a lot to me, but I didn't know how to make them mean anything to anyone else. It was important for me to try to do it, but I really was not succeeding for a long time." Her qualifier, "I wanted it to be well done," is a sentiment any of us writing about a beloved person can identify with.

Abbott didn't stop trying, though. In the late '90s, she created a website that organized the letters and diaries and photos and bits of her history with her father in a chronological way. "It sort of helped me to organize 'This is what our life's about' for myself." She started developing a book proposal. And in 2001, when she began her MFA program at the New School, in New York City, she wrote further into her story, and it became her thesis. "I wrote in these kind of lyrical, sort of present-tense moments, and my thesis was published as a chapbook, but it still didn't have an arc. It still wasn't really clear what the story was about, what it was doing. For me, it was just sort of a matter of 'this happened,' bearing witness to this, but not really interpreted, and any sort of meaning wasn't clear really."

She continued to write, and she published some essays in anthologies, but she still couldn't get her proposal to interest agents in a passionate way. For a while, she decided to take a break, and she put the project aside.

Meanwhile, her life was cracking wide open in other ways. She married writer and journalist Jeff Howe in 2004. In 2005, her daughter, Annabel, was born. Her son, Finn, arrived two years later.

She didn't give up on the idea of writing her book, however. During the 2009–2010 academic year, when Howe was completing a Nieman fellowship at Harvard, Abbott enrolled in classes that she thought might help her gain a broader perspective on her history. "One was a class on children's literature, and another was on '60s radical movements. I wanted to understand the times of my parents and to also understand children in stories," she explains.

These classes gave Abbott the historical frame she realized she needed for her book, the narrative arc that had been missing in her thesis. "When I was thinking about writing in '94 or '99 or 2005, the culture was at a very different place than it was by 2010. At that point, gay bullying had become a national news story. Gay marriage had become a national news story. This wasn't so much a fringe story anymore. And so, I felt like at that point that the story was bigger than me, that there was something larger I could tell."

Abbott also felt like she had firsthand knowledge of a point in time that many people did not have. "They could be allies and fight for these rights, and there could be representations of gay dads on TV, but I felt that there was this history that people just didn't know."

At the end of her husband's fellowship year, Abbott had the opportunity to pitch her story to agents and editors. They also embraced her perspective that the broader historical context woven into her personal experience was important and fascinating. She signed with an agent, wrote a new proposal, and sold the book that fall.

So, in 2011, she finally got to work on the story that she'd been thinking about for twenty years. "I was doing research and writing at the same time. Research, like reading through my dad's journals, reading through other books, looking through news clippings or watching documentaries, and sort of building up files of notes that were interesting to me on each decade and thinking about how to bring those together. I also decided that I would do kind of a parallel story, watching my dad's evolution, his struggles and changes against my evolution, my struggles and changes. Our stories were linked to each other, but also linked to San Francisco, linked to what was going on in gay rights."

"What was it like for you to discover all of that history and position it next to your own story?"

"There was definitely a lot of unprocessed grief. I took it on for the first time. When I was living through the history, obviously we didn't know it was history because it was the present, and a lot of it was just sort of making our way through the days," she explains, her eyes alive and thoughtful. "It was only after the research I did, twenty years after the fact, twenty years after my dad died, twenty years after the height of this epidemic, that I realized the depth of the loss. The depth of the stories. It's hard enough to lose a parent, but to think about the circumstances of the disease and how it killed so many people so young, and how it tore apart these communities and these friends and these lovers and these families . . . " She takes a deep breath. "I had never been able to consider that before."

"How did you cope with uncovering all of that sadness?"

"I was often sort of driven intellectually, because the process of doing research gives one the sense of traveling through time and asking, 'What was that time like?' I was curious, and it was interesting." But then there would be discoveries she'd make about her father and his illness that would force her to stop and take it all in. "In those instances," Abbott says, "I was just side-swiped emotionally."

She shares one of these moments. "I had never known when my dad had seroconverted [when the HIV antibody became detectable in his blood], and I was reading early reports on AIDS and how it worked throughout the body and thinking about when he might have been sick, and I might not have known it. Or when he might have been HIV positive, and he didn't know it. I'd find these correlations with his journals—like when he was tired—and my inability to sort of see that or respond to it. That was really painful, because I felt like that might have been going on and I didn't know. That was something new. That wasn't something that I felt so prepared for."

Abbott knew she needed to be alone in that grief, because it was such an intensity of new feeling for her. However, she also had two young children to take care of. "It was hard because I would have these hours of the day that I could be in this space, and then I would have to come home and put all that away."

Earning a Ragdale fellowship gave her the opportunity to do a three-week writing retreat in Lake Forest, Illinois. By taking this intentional time, she allowed herself to escape the other demands in her life and to stay in that emotional space. "I could be alone and cry and then go into the woods and not be constricted. A lot of that was just a release that I wasn't able to have before."

For Abbott, experiencing these acute feelings of loss could, at times, be overwhelming and frightening, but there was also something about them that she welcomed. They made her feel more closely connected to the story and to her dad. "There's a chapter where I focus more on the letters and that year and the relationship through letters and how it changed our relationship. In rereading those letters, I felt so close to my dad and so much love from him. That was hard because it just made me miss him more. But I also felt like for me this was such a full and satisfying experience of love, just to feel so loved by someone in that way that only a child can be loved. I just really, really wanted to capture my dad's voice and his particular form of love. Just his honesty."

In the chapter Abbott's referencing in *Fairyland*, there's a segment of one of her father's letters to her that begins, "Yesterday I was thinking you're the only person I love. Others I'm only fond of from time to time." These authentic reminders gave Abbott a fuller appreciation for her father. "He was a complicated guy. He could be cranky and obsessive or intellectual or know-it-all or flaky or whatever things, but I always trusted his presence in my life and that his love was really true. That he was rooting for me, and that he believed in me. I missed having someone in my life who loved that way. That was a really hard thing to take on and try to write about."

Abbott acknowledges that in some ways she'd taught herself to "normalize" her loss, to distance herself from it and make it rational and controlled. She'd told aspects of her story enough times over the years that the narrative had ceased to be so difficult.

"But," she explains, "there would be these kind of moments that were hidden away, pockets that were still very tender and raw. I liked having those because it would be like, 'Oh yeah, this is really sad,' or 'I am really sad about this and that's good.' I'm feeling something that's real, and it's powerful."

Historically, Abbott tells me, she was not a crier. "As a memoirist, I feel like I don't want to be sentimental. I don't want to be maudlin. I don't want to be self-pitying. So making it artful sometimes meant making it nonemotional, but then there were other times when my writing failed because it was not emotional enough." She had to find a balance. "I would sometimes have to work off of different channels. So there was one channel where I was sort of progressing through the outline and saying, 'This is what comes next.' And I had another channel where I just wrote reflections or moments of being that didn't have an intellectual purpose yet—significant moments for me that I just tried to write as vividly as possible."

This blend of straightforward chronological narrative and lovingly rendered scenes is what makes *Fairyland* such a powerful read. When I say this to Abbott, though, she's honest about some of the doubts she still carries about her approach. "Sometimes I wonder, Did I make it too chronological? Should I have made it more experimental? Or more memoir-like by challenging its shape and style?" Ultimately, she made the decision that she felt would give her readers the most access to the story. "My feeling with my story was that there were so many aspects to it that were hard for people to relate to. I wanted them to care about this history, even if they had no personal experience with it."

"How much of the writing did you share with others during the process?"

Abbott felt there were certain parts of her story that she needed to fact check. "I shared some of the chapters about the poetry movement in San Francisco with some of my dad's colleagues and other writers so they could say, 'I don't know if you should write about that,' or 'Yeah, I think you got that pretty right.'"

The exclusive relationship that Abbott had with her father, though, made her process different than what many writers who venture to tell family stories often face. "With my dad, I had license in our relationship. I felt like I had him to myself. Others have siblings and mothers and more complicated relationships." Abbott didn't have to think about protecting her father's privacy or defend her need to share the story. "I had full access," she says. "He was so open with me in his life. He wasn't the type who would say, 'I don't want you to write about me.'"

Except for a few sections where she describes visits to her grandparents' home and feeling like "some sort of weirdo orphan" when she was there, Abbott does not write at length about her extended family. "I thought about writing more about my grandmother or my mother, but that would have required me to interview family members, and it would be more of an act of imagination. I feel like I shared those people with my other family members, so they all have their own narrative, and it's much more tense." She says she only shared those sections with a couple of people in her family, to make sure she had done justice to these people she knew so little about.

In the end, Abbott understood that the book she'd carried inside her for so long was a father-daughter story. "This is the story that defined my whole life," she says. "I was always this girl with this story. This girl who lost her dad."

"What was it like for you to finish it?" I ask, running my hand over my tattered copy of *Fairyland* resting on the table between us.

"It was really hard for me to let it go because I actually enjoyed more writing the book than having the book written." She reiterates the way the process of writing had given her the gift of time travel and the chance to be with her dad. "To have the book written meant I couldn't make any changes to it. It couldn't be all potential. Now it was going to go out, and people were going to judge it. And judge me and judge him. And there was nothing I could do about it."

By verbalizing this fear of judgment, Abbott has linked to the universal anxiety of writing memoir. "How did you deal with these inevitable uncertainties?" I ask.

She's candid about the fact that, at first, she didn't deal well. "It was very easy for me to focus on whatever negative stuff I got. I used to read reader reviews on Amazon and Goodreads, and I would read them because I wanted to read the good stuff, but then I would inevitably read the bad stuff, and it would make me feel really awful. It became an exercise in ego lifting or ego bashing, and it was ultimately for nothing. It wasn't something I could respond to or address. So, I just stopped reading them completely, and that felt much better."

Abbott also feared the possibility that her story might just be ordinary. "There were moments even before I published the book where I questioned, 'Is this going to be the same story as someone else's?' The uniqueness of my story feels like its redemptive quality. And as hard as it is, no one has a story like it. I had a lot invested in this idea of its total extraordinariness, and so anything that would make it less than that was frightening."

To combat these doubts during the writing and after the book was published, Abbott says she thought of writing about events like the Holocaust. "There are so many Holocaust stories, but each one is different, each perspective, each regional distance. They are responding to the same horrible moment that was traumatic, but we don't say, 'Well, I already read the Holocaust story.' I felt like the same has to be true with AIDS." She chuckles. "People aren't going to say, 'Well, we did the AIDS book. AIDS doesn't sell.'"

Abbott also learned to moderate her expectations for the book. "I had to tell myself not to think, 'It has to win a National Book Critics Circle Award, and if it doesn't, it's a failure. If it's not on the *New York Times* best-seller list, it's a failure.'" She decided that she'd judge the success of her book on whether readers could say that her writing had helped them to know her father. "I just wanted people to love him to some degree the way I loved him."

Fairyland does make people love Steve Abbott, and it does make people care about the history in which he lived. And these qualities, wrapped in her precise and moving prose, have earned Abbott's memoir well-deserved critical praise. Published in 2013, *Fairyland* was named a *New York Times* "Editor's Choice," "A Book to Watch Out For" by the *New Yorker*, an *Oprah Magazine* "Book of the Week," and a "Best Book of 2013" by the *San Francisco Chronicle*. The book won the American Library Association's Stonewall Book Award and was a finalist for a Lambda Literary Award. *Fairyland* has been translated into French and Polish. It will also soon be published in Italian, Portuguese, and Spanish. Academy Award–winning screenwriter Sofia Coppola has acquired the film rights and is making the book into a movie.

The public acclaim for *Fairyland* has been important for Abbott, but the diverse and far-reaching personal connections the book has forged for her have been the most gratifying. "I would get e-mails from people saying, 'Oh, I had a gay dad too,' or, 'I had a dad who died of AIDS too, and this really meant a lot to me.' But there were also people who said, 'I used to work in theater, and your book reminded me of these guys I knew.'"

Fairyland speaks to the hidden history of AIDS—the collective loss from an epidemic that people didn't necessarily have a way to connect with. "I knew I was shining a light on a community that hadn't really been written about. The book helped them feel that again and remember those people and those times."

Fairyland has also reconnected Abbott with the gay community in a profound way. She tells me about responses from young gay men who've said, "I feel like I learned about my history now. What it means to be gay." Her voice is filled with emotion. "When my dad died, I felt like a refugee from the queer community. In writing this book, I wanted to say, 'Look, here I am. I care about this. This is my history and my culture as much as anything, and I want to be a part of it.' So for people to say, 'I feel you are a part of it,' that was a big, big deal for me."

She says of the book, "I'd wanted to create something that I felt like had lasting value, that I felt could reach a lot of people. I feel like it came out at the right time. I feel like a lot of people responded to it."

Among the many people who've responded to Abbott's story is a growing group like me: children who lost one or both parents to AIDS.

While Abbott was conducting research for *Fairyland*, she'd uncovered a staggering statistic. In 1992, the year her own father died, AIDS was the leading cause of death for men ages eighteen to forty-five. "I absorbed that, and thought, that's crazy," she says. "But I also thought, I bet a lot of those men were dads. Where are those stories?"

A decade earlier, she'd met Whitney Joiner, a features editor at *Marie Claire* magazine, and a daughter who'd also lost her father to AIDS in 1992. Joiner's experience was significantly different from Abbott's. Joiner's father remained closeted until his death, and when he died, her mother instructed her to tell people her father had died of cancer. The stigma of HIV/AIDS at the height of the epidemic had silenced the voices of many children, including me, whose parents fell victim to the disease. A stigma that left us isolated in our grief.

Abbott and Joiner wanted to bring these stories out of the shadows, so they created the Recollectors, an online community where children who'd lost parents to AIDS might connect and share their stories. Through essays and oral histories, the 175 (a number that continues to grow) members of the Recollectors are finding our voices and long-needed support from others who understand pieces of our experiences. The Recollectors have partnered with StoryCorps, a nonprofit organization committed to recording, preserving, and sharing the stories of ordinary people. Many of my fellow Recollectors have sat down with StoryCorps to share their experiences for the very first time of losing a parent or parents to AIDS.

"We've gotten terrific press, terrific response," Abbott tells me. "The stories themselves are amazing. You know, I needed to finish *Fairyland* because I needed to get beyond that story to tell other stories. It's been really powerful for me to tell those other stories. The occasions when I've written people's oral histories, I've felt profoundly invested in those stories. Very moved and proud. Knowing these stories is important. They are complicated, and they are beautiful in their complications."

Abbott allied me with the Recollectors after our first lunch in Boston. She's also invited me to write a piece for the website. In six months' time, at a Recollectors event in New York City to commemorate World AIDS Day, I will stand at the front of a room filled with strangers, fellow Recollectors, whose stories mirror mine in so many ways, and read the essay I'll write. The experience will be one of the most profound of my life.

As we wrap up today, I tell Abbott how meaningful it is to have this supportive space of the Recollectors' community after keeping my story and the vulnerable emotions that go with it to myself for so long. I credit her gutsy approach to writing *Fairyland* for helping to pave the way for many of us to begin loosening our grips on these memories we've held so tightly.

She smiles. "It makes me really happy to connect people and see them having friendships with each other. Through the site, people are starting to talk about this now. Stories they've never talked about before. And I do sincerely believe that for these people to talk about it publically is a form of activism. It's healing. We are saying, 'This happened and I'm not afraid to talk about it anymore. This is not my dad's story or my mom's story. This is my story now.'"

CHAPTER 18

Kim Stafford

· *100 Tricks Every Boy Can Do: How My Brother Disappeared*

There was no way I was going to complete this quest that he'd inspired without trying to somehow redeem my failed interaction with author, poet, and musician Kim Stafford. Soon after hearing him speak in Boston, I read his memoir, *100 Tricks Every Boy Can Do: How My Brother Disappeared*, a mosaic of beautiful vignettes pieced together to trek through the mystery of his brother's suicide and Stafford's attempt to answer the riddle of his brother's life. The resolution, though, is in the voyage, which helps Stafford understand his own life and live it more authentically. In the book's afterword, he writes: "This is a book of questions, a beginning—not a last word, or an end. [. . .] Where sorrow came like a wheeled vessel, and took my brother away (violence, blood, silence), memory and this telling bring him partway back."

And because I loved his approach to this complex story of grief, because I inherently understood how difficult it must have been to write, and because I saw glimpses of my own family in his brief portraits of his, I latched on even tighter to the idea of connecting with Stafford in some way.

Making that connection seems like a long shot since I have no personal contact information for Stafford, and his home is in Portland, Oregon. A Google search helps me finally find a faculty e-mail address for him through Lewis and Clark College, a private liberal arts college, where he teaches, directs the Northwest Writing Institute, and codirects the Documentary Studies Program. I know how easily messages get lost in my own faculty inbox, so I am not counting on a quick response when I send Stafford my pitch letter.

To my surprise and delight, he responds the next day. As it turns out, I've intersected with Kim Stafford at a monumental time. The year 2014 marks the hundredth birthday of his late father, renowned American poet William Stafford. In remembrance of his father's life and lasting literary legacy, Kim Stafford, literary executor of the William Stafford archives, is immersed in a yearlong series of events, exhibitions, symposiums, tributes, and publications throughout the state of Oregon.

The William Stafford Centennial Celebration has "taken over my life," Stafford writes in his return e-mail, and he has just "slivers of time." There's no hyperbole in the way Stafford characterizes his schedule. I discover through a little research of my own that this Centennial Celebration is an enormous undertaking, and Kim Stafford is a featured guest reader/speaker at many of the events listed on the "2014 Stafford Centennial Calendar" that I find online. This itinerary, added to his teaching and writing, makes him a very busy man. Despite how busy he is, he graciously invites me to send him my questions about his memoir.

I know my window of opportunity is small, so I forward my questions to him that same day. And this time, because I'd actually "rehearsed" what to ask him, I get a lot closer to the answers I'm looking for when it comes to surviving the writing of hard stories.

Stafford says there was "a delay of decades" before he managed to tell the hard story of his brother's suicide in a way that felt manageable. In 1988, at forty years old, Bret Stafford shot himself. *One Hundred Tricks Every Boy Can Do* was published in

2012. Stafford describes what eventually prompted him to write: "I realized I needed to understand my brother's life in order to be a better father as our son began to come of age. I advance my understanding by writing. But," Stafford reveals, "I wrestled with how to tell it at every stage.

When Stafford recognized that understanding Bret's story meant looking at all the fragments that shaped it, he was finally able to write it. "As I tell in the opening page of the book, during a conversation with my son I had a vision of 'a parade of enigmatic moments from childhood through our years together and beyond.' I realized this sequence of scenes would have to become a book."

In his essay "How a Book Can Set You Free," published on the *Northwest Book Lover's* blog, the same essay he'd read from that snowy day in Boston—Stafford further explains: "In this case, the whole story had seemed impossible to tell, too big and too strange. This story had been a silence in my family for twenty-four years. Only by telling it in little sips, some half a page, some half a dozen pages, could I bring it forth at last. Brief acts of witness for the writer, compact glimpses for the reader—together, these had gathered into the book in my hands."

Stafford's piecing together of "compact glimpses" is strikingly similar to how Joan Wickersham's story of her father's suicide emerged by looking at it "thing by thing." And both authors illuminate what perhaps we all need to understand when looking at our complicated stories: trying to see them as wholes, without first examining their parts, doesn't necessarily work.

"I went into myself, and I wrote," Stafford says of his process to bring the various parts of his story to the page. "The more mysterious dimensions of the story were the ones I most needed to tell, or try to tell."

One of those mysterious dimensions is what he describes as "the silence in my father's practice, and my family's culture, when things get hard." Heartbreakingly, Stafford's father, the celebrated man of words, never spoke with him about Bret's death. "He could not speak with us about the puzzle of his own dead son, his fears, the dense interior of his pain. Or as he says in his one poem about my brother, 'Why tell what hurts?'" Stafford writes. The rest of the Stafford family followed that lead, and much of their grief went unspoken long after William Stafford, their standard-bearer, was gone.

In writing this memoir, Kim Stafford was forced to confront and challenge his family's culture of silence. "Some passages that I imagined might be painful for my family gave me pause."

"How did you find the courage to keep moving through them when those doubts crept in?" I ask.

"It wasn't a matter of courage at that point. A chapter late in the book, titled 'Kuleana,' attempts to respond to this question. *Kuleana* is the Hawaiian word for responsibility. It tells how each of us will come into possession of certain stories, and it is our right—and our responsibility—to decide which stories to tell, how to tell them, to whom we may tell them, and why. These considerations were at play every day I was writing. Finally, it came to me that 'if we are silent about the story of someone dear to us, silence will be the story of that person.' I was not willing to let silence be the final story of my brother."

Stafford did offer to let his mother, sisters, and brother's two children read the manuscript before it was published. "They opted to wait," he says. "When my mother first read the book, she had a classic response: 'Socrates said the unexamined life is not worth living, but after reading your book, I wonder if the over-examined life is not worth living, either.' But then after I gave my first public reading from the book, she burst out, 'Well that was fun! Those were good stories!'"

Of other family responses, Stafford says, "My brother's daughter told me, kindly, that I was too hard on myself in the book: 'You couldn't have saved my dad. He was on a path of his own.'"

Readers outside Stafford's family were generous and kind in their reactions to the memoir. "Responses ranged from full discussion and appreciation, to tears and sorrow, and everything in between." Stafford wasn't sure exactly how to react himself. "I was helpless in responding. I knew there would be a range of responses, but I knew I just had to write the book."

Stafford also discovered something else. "Once the book was published, I realized a new ambition for the project: I don't want the book to be so much the story of a suicide as a model for how others might tell a difficult story in many short chapters. My formulation for this process, as I've articulated it to describe a workshop I do, goes like this: 'One can compose a work of any length or difficulty, given writing solitudes of any brevity, by designing a cell-like structure that empowers steady progress toward a worthy goal.' I would like to see this book act as an 'Open Sesame!' for others who have kept long silence about a story that could be told in some form like this book."

I ask whether the pursuit of this ambition impacted Stafford's sense of ownership over the story and his way of telling it. He says no. "As I said in the afterword: 'There is no way I can tell my brother's story. That would be the work of the many who knew him. Instead, I write my stories of my brother. These are the stories that are mine to tell.' I have to own my stories of my brother. The story of my brother remains in the world beyond me."

After reading Stafford's book, reading the essay he wrote about his book, and reading his answers to my questions, I recognize that the biggest impact of his memoir does not rest in what it might have done for readers but instead what it has done for Stafford. He says he began writing with a simple ambition: "I missed my brother and wanted to reconnect with him by writing his story." The rewards of the process gave him something bigger, though. "In practice, by writing I learned how to remember. That is, as I wrote, more came to me than I had known. The act of writing recreated my brother in my mind, and he moved from a sorrowful shadow to a vibrant character."

In writing *100 Tricks Every Boy Can Do*, Stafford performed his own stirring trick. He made his brother reappear. He says he did it by "reach[ing] back through the difficult ending, to grasp the beautiful beginning—like pulling a venomous serpent inside out."

I cling to this idea with the same ferocity I clung to the lines about the stone that was no longer harnessed to Stafford's heart that he read from his essay at the Association of Writers and Writing Programs conference in Boston. I understand that my father's illness and death eclipsed him and buried me. Now, by writing through the pieces of my hard story, I am trying to dig myself out. Stafford's experience ignites my faith that somewhere in that digging, I just might rediscover my father, too.

Afterword

A year ago this week, a dear friend's husband was killed on impact when their SUV slid on an icy patch of New Hampshire highway, rolled, and crushed his side of the car. The next afternoon, I stood with my friend in her bedroom in an unbearable moment so heavy with grief it felt difficult to breathe and listened while she talked to her son and daughter, fifteen and twelve, about going to the funeral home to see their dad's body one final time. To say good-bye.

While his sister sobbed openly, my friend's son stood stoic, his arms held tight across his chest, his jaw clenched. I watched him struggle to contain the agony I knew he must feel. I reached out my hand, gently touched his arm and said, "It's okay to cry, Bud. This is sad. You can cry. You don't have to do this by yourself." I felt his body lean into my palm. His arms loosened. His shoulders sagged. And his face softened as tears began to trail down his cheeks.

The worst story that we can tell ourselves is that we are alone.

Human experience is universal though the specifics might vary. On the day I stood watching my friend's son confront the impossible grief in that moment of losing his father, the grief I'd felt when I lost mine entered that room. My loss connected to his, and I knew that in that intersection, I had comfort to offer.

When I sat down to interview the memoirists for this book, each one held out the same cup of comfort for me. They'd been where I was in my writing journey. They'd felt similar fears about committing their hard stories to the page, and they knew that I needed to hear that what I was feeling was okay. Normal. Even expected.

During a presentation I attended at the Miami Book Fair, Mary Karr—author of three best-selling memoirs and the 2015 *Art of Memoir*, a uniquely personal exploration of the genre—said, "Writing memoir, if it's done right, is like knocking yourself out with your own fist." In one sentence, she summed up what we all discover when we venture into this territory: writing hard stories is excruciatingly hard work.

The lesson I learned, though, from my two years talking with writers who've done that hard work, in some cases more than once, is that carrying around the terrible weight of hard stories without ever seeking a way to transform it into something lighter—even something beautiful—is a whole lot harder.

Author and counselor Allan Hunter, a firm believer in and practitioner of narrative therapy, wrote a book called *Write Your Memoir: The Soul Work of Telling Your Story*. At the beginning of this quest, I was privileged to spend an afternoon with him at his home in Watertown, Massachusetts. Among the many wonderful insights he shared that day was this: "Pain is like a little stone. If you put it in your pocket, it weighs nothing at all. If you put it inside your shoe, it will cripple you. The same little bit of pain. Where are you going to wear it?" In his book and his practice, Hunter advocates writing memoir to help us to shift the weight of our pain. "You are moving the grief from where it is doing no good to the place where you can carry it more easily."

But Hunter also understands that though the composition process is solitary and finding the voice with which to tell our stories is solitary, facing the traumas in our stories need not be. He ended our conversation that day with the story of Dante's journey into Hell in *The Divine Comedy*. "He goes to edge of the most terrifying and painful thing he can imagine—the devil himself, frozen in place. But he's not alone. Virgil guides him. And he is kept completely safe."

I found my Virgil in each one of the authors who spoke with me for this project. Collectively, they took me by the hand and said, "Come with me. The trip might be scary, but don't worry. I've been to where you are going. I know the way."

Their words buoyed me and nudged me back to my desk, back to that blinking cursor on my laptop screen. Their voices drowned out the noise of my fears, and I felt a newfound courage to continue writing into my story. While I completed this book, I also finished my creative thesis—two-thirds of my memoir—and received my MFA. I've found a rhythm to my writing and I know where I'm headed. The memoir isn't finished, but for the first time really, I believe that it will be. Soon.

At the beginning of my memoir-writing journey, I set out to put my story to rest. I really thought it was something that I needed to let go. But, now, I can echo the insights and wisdom of the writers in this book: Writing through the experience has, instead, offered me something tangible that I want to hold on to. By giving its pieces words and contour and structure and meaning, I've learned that I can take that crippling pebble out of my shoe and start finding other places to wear it.

This is the passage through which any one of us who is experiencing or has experienced trauma can travel. A more finite way to come to terms with our stories. If we're writers, *coming to terms* is exactly what we do. We find language to unravel the complexities of what happened, and we re-stitch those complexities into narratives that can become meaningful to others. And those are the narratives that have the potential to give others the courage to find their own.

Acknowledgments

Heartfelt thanks to the memoirists profiled in these pages. Their stunning books inspired my quest for companionship while writing my own memoir, and their amazing generosity of time and words opened the door for the creation of this book.

Deep appreciation to the good people who believed in this book and helped me navigate the unfamiliar territory of publishing it, especially my agent, John Talbot, and my editor, Helene Atwan. For their wonderful design work and copyediting, my thanks to the talented production team at Beacon Press.

I am profoundly grateful to the friends and family members who walked alongside me throughout this particular writing journey. Suzanne Strempek Shea championed this project from the beginning with boundless encouragement, feedback, and advice. I could not ask for a better mentor or dearer friend. To my close friends who are also writers—Danara Wallace, Jennifer Dupree, Philip Osgood, Sarah Church Baldwin, Amanda Pleau, Betsy Small Campbell, and Amanda Silva—thank you for pushing me on and understanding the angst of it all. For their support and love, thanks to Shayna Burgher, Meg Gould, Gretchen Warsen, Mindy Scales, Madeleine Lauzon-Dockrill, Sharon D'Errico, and Beth Barker. To my brave friend Hillari Wennerstrom, whose own very hard story intersected with the writing of this book, deepening my empathy and giving me an intimate glimpse into why the words shared in these pages have value beyond the writing community. Special thanks to dear friends Julie and Geoff Norris, who gave me the much-needed gift of space and tranquility in the final weeks of writing this manuscript by offering me their beautiful house on the beach in York, Maine. For his help in quieting my deepest insecurities and keeping my mental health somewhat intact, my sincerest thanks to Dr. Tim Bray.

And, finally, to my mother, brothers, sisters-in-law, brothers-in-law, mother-in-law, and father-in-law, I am consistently thankful for the knowledge that you are always just a phone call away to encourage and support when I need you.

About the Author

Melanie Brooks is a writer, teacher, and mother living in Nashua, New Hampshire, with her husband, two children, and yellow Lab. She received her MFA in creative nonfiction from the University of Southern Maine's Stonecoast Master's in Fine Arts program. She teaches college writing at Northeastern University in Boston, Massachusetts, and Merrimack College in Andover, Massachusetts. She also teaches creative writing at Nashua Community College in New Hampshire. Her work has appeared in *Hippocampus*, *The Huffington Post*, *Modern Loss*, *Solstice Literary Magazine*, *The Recollectors*, *Stonecoast Review*, *Washington Post*, and *Word Riot*. Her almost completed memoir explores the devastating impact of living with the ten-year secret of her father's HIV infection before his death in 1995. Brooks's writing is the vehicle through which she's starting to understand that impact.

Helen Peppe Photography